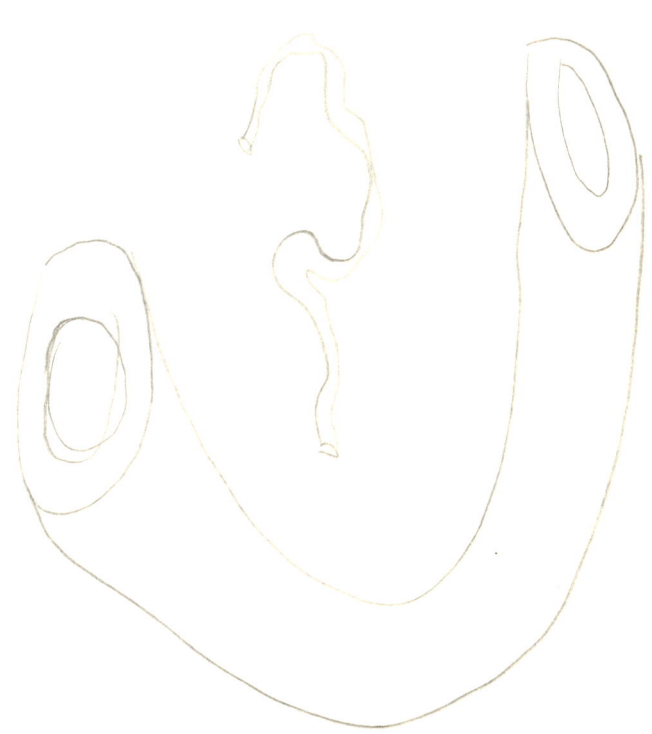

LET'S CELEBRATE CHRISTMAS!

BY THE SAME AUTHOR

*

LET'S CELEBRATE CHRISTMAS!

HAPPY BIRTHDAY TO YOU!

GAMES AND STUNTS FOR ALL OCCASIONS

THE YEAR 'ROUND PARTY BOOK

COURTESY BOOK

BOTH SIDES OF THE MICROPHONE

THE BOOK OF ORIGINAL PLAYS AND
HOW TO GIVE THEM

LET'S CELEBRATE CHRISTMAS

*

PARTIES PLAYS LEGENDS
CAROLS POETRY STORIES

*

HORACE J. GARDNER

*
* *
*

Illustrated by Edna Potter

THE RONALD PRESS COMPANY
NEW YORK

COPYRIGHT, 1940, 1950, BY HORACE J. GARDNER
ALL RIGHTS RESERVED

Copyright renewed © 1968 by Mildred R. Gardner

GT
4985
.G3
1968

*

The text of this publication, or any part thereof may not be reproduced in any manner whatsoever without permission in writing from the owner of the copyright.

16MP

157439

Library of Congress Catalog Card Number: 56-12830
PRINTED IN THE UNITED STATES OF AMERICA

AFFECTIONATELY DEDICATED TO
HER
WHOSE HELP AND INSPIRATION
HAVE ENCOURAGED ME
TO WRITE MANY BOOKS

CONTENTS

Introduction	*Let's Celebrate Christmas!*	ix
I	The Greatest Christmas Story Ever Told	1
II	From a Christmas Scrapbook	5

    Symbols of Christmas
    Legends and Customs
        In England, France, Germany, Italy, Spain, Switzerland, Russia, Rumania, Denmark, Belgium, Finland, Brazil, Mexico.

III	Christmas Today in Other Lands	25

        In England, France, Germany, Italy, Russia, Finland, Denmark, Switzerland, Rumania, Belgium, Dominican Republic, Brazil, Mexico, Sweden.

IV	The Christmas Party	41

    The Home-coming Party
    Games
        Ice Breakers, Pencil and Pad Pastimes, The Life of the Party, Christmas Quizzes
    Games and Parties for Children
        An Old-Fashioned Children's Party
        Four-to-Six-Year Groups
        Seven-to-Eleven-Year Groups
        Twelve-to-Fifteen-Year Groups
        Mrs. Santa Claus' Reception
    Decorations
    Refreshments

V	Christmas Carols	87

    Cradle Hymn
    It Came Upon the Midnight Clear
    Good King Wenceslas
    Christmas Eve

Songs of Praise the Angels Sang
O Come, All Ye Faithful
Joy to the World
Hark! The Herald Angels Sing
Silent Night
O Little Town of Bethlehem
We Three Kings of Orient
The First Noel
Once in Royal David's City
God Rest You Merry, Gentlemen
Good Christian Men, Rejoice

VI CHRISTMAS PLAYS   105
    Christmas Treasure
    Reunion at Christmas

VII CHRISTMAS POETRY AND STORIES   155
    Christmas: A Definition by Clement A. Miles
    Is There a Santa Claus by Francis P. Church
    At Bracebridge Hall by Washington Irving
    The Fir Tree by Hans Christian Andersen
    Christmas at Thunder Gap by Katharine O. Wright
    The Festival of Saint Nicholas
                           by Mary Mapes Dodge
    The Night Before Christmas by Clement C. Moore
    Heigh Ho, The Holly! by William Shakespeare
    Minstrels by William Wordsworth
    Voices in the Mist by Alfred Lord Tennyson
    To a Child by Robert Herrick
    Let us Kneel with Mary Maid by Christina Rossetti
    Where is the Babe by Robert Herrick
    I Sing the Birth by Ben Jonson
    This! the Happy Morn by John Milton
    Stop Thief! by Robert Herrick
    Christmas—1863 by Henry Wadsworth Longfellow

INDEX   206

FOREWORD

ALL TOO often in these materialistic days, the commercial and social aspects of the Christmas season have tended to overwhelm the spiritual to the point where a sense of the significance of this greatest holiday of the Christian year is lost in a welter of shopping and parties. The bad effects of this attitude are felt both at home and at school. No wonder the Puritans, in order to restore to this sacred holiday its solemn dignity, forbade indulgence in all the forms of gaiety traditional to the observance of Christmas in their time.

Now and then one runs across a sort of sane and sensible (as well as sensitive) formula, or calendar of faith, that can be helpful in saving Christmas for Christmas' sake. For unless Christmas means a pause to remember that the teachings of Christ are important to us today, there is no such thing as "Christmas spirit." In that case the event may as well be yielded up to commercial interests, as were flowers when we began to "say it" with them, as were Christmas cards when people began selling them for pin money, as was love when it went off to Hollywood.

So the other day I took heart when I met the book *Let's Celebrate Christmas*. Here, I said, is a forward step in the right direction. For with this book, one can lay a complete course for the celebration of the days before Christmas for the home and community that will bring us to the manger in a sincere mood of peace on earth, good will among men.

For instance, one may select from this book several ceremonial customs of foreign lands, one for each day, that not only would stir the child's ready imagination, but also teach him that all nations do not honor Christmas in the same ways: the ring ceremony from Russia, the Roumanian blessing of the trees, the singing of the German cradle songs, the Swiss peeling of the onions, the lighting of the oil lamps in Spain as the first star appears in the evening sky. And, also to make us further aware of international differences that are interesting, *because* differences are interesting, there are several pages here of Christmas recipes, including the particularities of an American Christmas dinner. Here are poems that can easily be memorized and recited in the classroom, at the church program, as grace before supper, children and adults in unison: Herrick's "Where is the Babe?", Ben Johnson's "I Sing the Birth," Longfellow's "Christmas—1863." Here are songs to be sung in school, around the neighborhood, by candlelight, by the family and community: Martin Luther's "Cradle Hymn," Isaac Watt's "Joy to the World," John Hopkins' "We Three Kings of Orient Are." There are plays, too, that can be learned and presented by the children. And stories that can be read parent to child, teacher to pupil.

Here, indeed, is enough material to build a crèche around the idea of Christmas. All we need do, for at least the *week* before Christmas, is refrain from the market place, abstain a little from social convention, go not apart from home and church, family and closest friends, learn (by heart) a song and poem from Horace Gardner's *Let's Celebrate Christmas,* and we might well be following the Star again.

LESLEY FROST

LET'S CELEBRATE CHRISTMAS!

CHAPTER I

THE GREATEST CHRISTMAS STORY EVER TOLD

AND IT came to pass in those days, that there went out a decree from Cæsar Augustus, that all the world should be taxed. (*And* this taxing was first made when Cyrenius was governor of Syria.)

And all went to be taxed, every one into his own city.

And Joseph also went up from Galilee, out of the city of Nazareth, into Judæa unto the city of David, which is called Bethlehem; (because he was of the house and lineage of David).

To be taxed with Mary his espoused wife, being great with child.

And so it was, that, while they were there, the days were accomplished that she should be delivered.

And she brought forth her firstborn son, and wrapped him in swaddling clothes, and laid him in a manger; because there was no room for them in the inn.

And there were in the same country shepherds abiding in the field, keeping watch over their flock by night.

And, lo, the angel of the Lord came upon them, and the glory of the Lord shone round about them: and they were sore afraid.

And the angel said unto them, Fear not: for, behold, I bring you good tidings of great joy, which shall be to all people.

For unto you is born this day in the city of David a Saviour, which is Christ the Lord.

And this *shall be* a sign unto you; Ye shall find the babe wrapped in swaddling clothes, lying in a manger.

And suddenly there was with the angel a multitude of the heavenly host, praising God, and saying,

Glory to God in the highest, and on earth peace, good will toward men.

And it came to pass, as the angels were gone away from them into heaven, the shepherds said one to another, Let us now go even unto Bethlehem, and see this thing which is come to pass, which the Lord hath made known unto us.

And they came with haste, and found Mary and Joseph, and the babe lying in a manger.

And when they had seen *it*, they made known abroad the saying which was told them concerning this child.

And all they that heard *it* wondered at those things which were told them by the shepherds.

But Mary kept all these things, and pondered *them* in her heart.

And the shepherds returned, glorifying and praising God for all the things that they had heard and seen, as it was told unto them.

ST. LUKE 2:1-20.

CHAPTER II

FROM A CHRISTMAS SCRAPBOOK

TWENTY-FIVE YEARS ago the author wrote this paragraph in a notebook, which he recently discovered in complacent repose beneath a blanket of dust in the old attic bookcase: "Eight things are always associated with Christmas. First and foremost is its religious significance. The other seven are: hanging the mistletoe, burning the yule log, the Christmas tree, the Christmas carol, the greeting card, the Christmas stocking, and Santa Claus himself." Since that was written a quarter of a century ago the world has been in a whirlpool of change, but these eight symbols remain unchanged.

SYMBOLS OF CHRISTMAS

Religious Significance of Christmas

The anniversary of the birth of Jesus Christ is the greatest festival of the year, and is one of the few religious events observed by all His followers. Indeed, to all Christians the birthday of the Messiah shares with Easter the distinction of being one of the two most solemn events of all history.

One can hardly state definitely that December 25th is the right anniversary of Christ's nativity, for the early Christians thought it insulting to keep the birthday of Christ, "as if He were a king Pharaoh." This was because of the wild orgies held when the rulers of that time became a year older. However, the bacchanalian revels diminished as a series of depressions engulfed the pagan world. At the same time, Christianity was spreading in every civilized country. With its triumph, Church authorities began to dip into records to ascertain the exact date of the Nativity.

Writing in the fourth century, St. John Chrysostom tells us that

Julius, the Pope of Rome from 337 to 352, commissioned St. Cyril to make an investigation to determine the day and the month. Cyril learned that the Western churches were unanimous in celebrating the event on December 25th, but that all the Eastern churches did not agree with the Western units, nor with each other. Many of the Eastern churches kept January 6th as Christ's birthday, as well as the anniversary of His epiphany or manifestation through baptism, miracle, and the Star that led the Magi.

We are told that after considerable deliberation Pope Julius, in A.D. 350, established December 25th for the festival in Rome, but there is much discrepant testimony. It was nearly a hundred years later (A.D. 440) that it was established in Jerusalem. But both in the East and the West, December 25th had long been a great pagan festival of the winter solstice, when the retreating sun turns again, and renews the year, and the days begin to lengthen. It was a joyous feast, and the world needed joy. So it was that the pagan festival of the "unconquerable sun" gave way to the Christian festival of the true Sun which "lighteth every man who cometh into the world."

Hanging the Mistletoe

Many of the rites of the present-day American and English Christmas were carried over from pagan festivals when our forefathers became Christianized. Two of the most cherished are the hanging of the mistletoe and the burning of the yule log.

Legends say that the Druids regarded the mistletoe with utmost veneration, though this reverence seems to have been restricted to the plant when growing on an oak, the favorite tree of their god Tutanes. But some folklorists point to the Scandinavian rites and myths concerned with the mistletoe as having killed the sun-god, Baldur the Beautiful. Perhaps both are true, who knows? But we all do know that nowadays if a pretty girl steps under the mistletoe, —well, it is an invitation to exchange osculatory greetings.

The Yule Log's Glow

It is generally agreed that the burning of the yule log was handed down to English-speaking countries by our Scandinavian ancestors who, at the feast of the winter solstice, kindled huge bonfires in honor of their god Thor. In England, the bringing in and burning of the yule log on Christmas Eve was a pretty ceremony. The log usually included the root of a ponderous oak, which was drawn into the castle amid great noise and singing. The larger estates engaged minstrels to sing to the log, but where minstrels were not available, it was customary for each member of the family to take a turn in saluting the yule log with an appropriate song. And when at last the fire died out, the remnant of the log was put away until next yuletide, to kindle with it a new yule log.

The Christmas Tree—"Made in Germany"
Although various countries have impressive legends about the first Christmas tree, it is generally believed that the decorated pine or cedar, so popular in America and England today, is of German origin. Perhaps it harks back to the old heathen tree worship; perhaps to the medieval custom of welcoming guests with trees studded with candles, of which the minstrel Wolfram von Eschenbach sang in the thirteenth century; perhaps Martin Luther could claim the honor. There is the story, you will recall, of Luther deriving his inspiration for a tree from thousands of glittering stars one Christmas Eve. The Christmas tree was introduced into England just over one hundred years ago after the marriage of Queen Victoria to the German Prince Albert. Even before that the tree had been brought to America by German immigrants and the delightful custom was quickly taken up by the New World settlers of all nationalities.

The Christmas Carol
The carol, or Christmas song, was already popular before the fourteenth century, and it has retained this popularity through the succeeding centuries. Over a hundred old carols have survived and are now a definite part of most services held at Christmas. They are also kept alive from year to year by young people of the church who march in groups and peal out the inspiring melodies on Christmas Eve, as pauses are made in front of a neighbor's house or on the village street corners. In England, this singing of carols is an important part of the festival season. The singers, or "waits" as they are called, go from door to door and anticipate gifts of money in return for the sacred melodies. Recitals in Westminster Abbey, St. Paul's, and Temple Church in London are inspiring.

One of the most abidingly popular of all old English carols begins with this familiar stanza:

> "God rest you merry, Gentlemen,
> Let nothing you dismay,
> For Jesus Christ in Bethlehem
> Was born upon this day."

Christmas Greeting Cards

The first holiday greeting cards were mailed around the middle of the nineteenth century, and are of comparatively recent origin. The early ones were pen-flourishes simulating birds, scrolls and flowers, with the greeting beautifully written underneath the display of penmanship. In 1884 the London *Times* settled a controversy revolving around several artists who claimed to have published the first Christmas card. It was decided that Sir Henry Cole originated the idea, and that the first publisher was Joseph Cundall, a London artist, in 1846. About one thousand of these cards were sold. Greeting cards were not immediately popular, and not until 1862 did the custom begin to grow noticeably. Today, however, sending and receiving cards is one of the most delightful of all the holiday customs.

The Christmas Stocking

The use of stockings as a receptacle for gifts from Santa Claus can be traced to only one legend of long ago. The story goes that the jovial little driver of the reindeer dropped some gold coins down a chimney one night. Normally they would have fallen on the hearth, but instead, the money went into a stocking which had been left by the fireside to dry. Ever since that time, old Santa has been expected to fill any and all stockings he finds when he makes his nocturnal call. In some parts of Europe stockings are hung on St. Andrew's Day, November 30th, or for St. Befana to fill on Epiphany. In certain sections of France and Germany, the wooden shoes are put out to be filled, instead of the stocking.

Santa Claus

Most people don't know that Santa Claus is really a native of New York. The Dutch settlers brought him to New Amsterdam, as a pale-faced ascetic, dressed in his antique bishop's robes. But after New Amsterdam became New York, Clement Moore transformed the charitable saint—and I rather think St. Nicholas liked the change, too—into a rosy-cheeked, plump and jolly old man with reindeer and sleigh to bring presents to all good little boys and girls. And at the same time, he was promoted from his own December 6th to Christmas itself, or rather the Night Before Christmas.

His fame quickly spread to the homelands across the sea, and in Holland and Germany, as well as in England, he instantly became popular as the secret dispenser of holiday presents to young and old.

LEGENDS AND CUSTOMS

ENGLAND

In the Middle Ages

Christmas was a great Church festival, celebrated in medieval times by the King and his barons, by the clergy, and by practically nobody else. Gradually the observance became widespread, and by the time Henry VIII ascended the throne it was a red-letter day throughout the realm. Edward VI preserved its customs with great lavishness, as did Queen Elizabeth during the early part of her reign. The celebration lost some of its splendor toward the end of her rule, but it was restored when James I succeeded her in 1603. It is recorded that he disliked the boar's head, and substituted turkey at all Christmas feasts. Henry VIII may have introduced the turkey to the English table, but it was James who really made it popular.

Table Technique in Elizabethan Days

"In days of old, when knights were bold, and barons held their sway," the baron of beef rose huge on one end of the table, and the haunch of venison on the other, and in between the table groaned under the weight of enormous platters of meat and fish. A knight might use his knife-of-all-work to cut up the meat of the lady next him. (Even in mid-Victorian England a gentleman was supposed to cut up the meat for his fair partner!) But it was quite proper to eat with your fingers, and to dunk and sop up victuals with bread. There was little choice in the matter, for table knives and forks were a rather newfangled foreign affectation, and costly. Even Queen Elizabeth and her gourmand of a father had a quaint habit of tossing bones and scraps of meat over their shoulders to the hungry hounds which had sniffed their way into the feast. Instead of napkins, the diners dried their fingers on their garments, or waved them in the air. It is true that at banquets a basin of water was passed around, but hardly anyone used it at the Christmas board.

After perhaps nine hours of feasting, the Diamond Jim Bradys of the day would adjourn to the drawing room for a midnight snack, which might include a barrel of oysters with pheasants on the side, eased down the red lane by big bowls of steaming hot punch.

Following refreshments, a knight chosen by lot as the Master of Merry Disports usually appointed a Lord of Misrule who led the sports and games program. Sometimes his sway was for the one night, but sometimes until New Year's or even Twelfth Night (January 6th); his authority was almost absolute, and he was usually a practical joker—the humor of the times was robust!

Gold Platters Preferred

The dish of the Christmas banquet was a peacock, brought in on a golden platter, its crested head erect and its tail gracefully outspread. And as a companion, it might have a boar's head, steaming hot, bedecked with savory herbs, and with an apple between its gleaming teeth. It was a sight to warm the cockles of the heart, this dish all garnished with sprigs of rosemary, and followed by other platters of jugged hare, roast turkey, beef and mince pies.

You have heard the story of the Christmas dinner Queen Elizabeth tendered in honor of the Duc d'Anjou? There was an international alliance involved, most important to the Virgin Queen, and she was doing her utmost to impress the duke with the magnificence of her court and her possessions. The peacock was customarily brought in by a lady of the court—it was quite an honor to bear it in—. As the story goes, the peacock was on a silver platter instead of on a golden dish. The Tudors had bad tempers, and the Queen flew into a rage; she refused to allow the lady who had brought it in to marry the gentleman who carried the gravy boat;

and she didn't relent until nine months later. Even so, their little romance was not spoiled, though the Queen's projected French marriage and alliance came to nought.

Old English Customs Still in Being

The Devil's Knell is tolled at Dewsbury, even to this day. Hundreds of years ago a youth was killed and his body thrown into a stream. The murderer was discovered, and as a penance he gave a tenor bell to the Dewsbury parish church. The bell tolls once for each year that has passed since the birth of Christ.

An Ashen Fagot is ceremoniously burned each Christmas Eve at Dunster in Somersetshire, in commemoration of the battles in Wessex in 878, when the warriors warmed themselves at night by burning branches of the ash tree.

Old Christmas Day (January 6th) is celebrated at Haxey Hood, Haxey, near Doncaster. The story is of a noble lady who lost her hood in the wind while on the way to church. Laborers near by restored the headpiece, and as a reward she donated a piece of ground now known as the Hoodlands, so that a hood could be thrown into the air and fought for annually on Christmas Day. Legend has it that this game later developed into Rugby football.

Information, Please!

Again necessity proved to be the mother of invention, in the case of the English Christmas Pudding. An early English king went hunting the day before Christmas, and became lost in a blizzard which blocked the paths in the forest and compelled him and his followers to remain all night in the wilds. One of the party happened to be the cook, so he prepared the Christmas meal from what was on hand. He decided to throw everything he had into the pot, and hope for the best. So he took the remains of a stag killed the day before, chopped the meat fine and added flour, apples, dried plums, eggs, ale, meat, brandy and sugar. After stirring, he tied the sticky mass in a bag and boiled it until it was a pudding. The true English Christmas pudding of today has all of these ingredients.

Sir Walter Scott tells of the old English Wassail Bowl. Rowena, beautiful daughter of Hengist, presented Prince Vortigern with a bowl of wine, and saluted him with "Lord King, Wass-heil!" to which he answered, "Drinc-heile," and saluted her. He was captivated by her charms, and married her soon thereafter. In the vernacular of the U. S. A. "Wass-heil!" has been translated into, "Here's to you!"

Pantomimes of fairy tales are an indispensable part of Christmas in the theaters of London and the provincial cities of England, and so are the waits (the name seems to refer to the night street-watchmen of former times) who make the chill air sweet with their carol singing.

FRANCE

Le Jour de Noël

Some of the sweetest Christmas carols are French, but in France the *Jour de Noël* or Christmas Day is exclusively for boys and girls. Centuries ago the custom began of telling children how *le petit Jésus, Sauveur adorable, Le nuit de Noël* was born in a stable, and the children came to believe that on Christmas Eve the heavens would open and *Le Petit Noël* would come down to bring them presents, if they were good children. In more recent times *Le Petit Noël* has been replaced by *Le Père Noël*—Father Christmas—a heavenly personage who has charge of distributing toys and good things to well-behaved children. In many parts of France the children believe that *Le Père Noël* has a companion, *Le Père Fouettard*—Father Spanker—who carries a load of switches, a few of which he leaves for those children who have not been good.

The Yule Log is a favorite everywhere in France except in Paris, where central heating has done away with most of the fireplaces. To perpetuate the old custom, however, pastry cooks bake long cakes in the shape of logs, with a coating of chocolate cream to look like the bark. Elsewhere, the log is hauled from the forest by a team of oxen, is placed in the chimney, sprinkled with Holy Water, and the fire is started by the head of the house. It burns throughout Christmas Eve, and slowly cooks the repast which is enjoyed by the family when it returns from midnight Mass.

There is hardly a home in France without a miniature crèche or crib set, made of cardboard and representing Christ in the manger, with the surrounding characters. Sometimes a doll represents the infant Jesus in the crib, and colored statuettes stand for the Virgin Mary, St. Joseph, the Three Wise Men carrying gifts, and the shepherds. There is usually room for an ox and an ass, and at least one or two sheep and lambs. The guiding star gleams brightly above, and sometimes a stately camel follows the adoring Magi.

Le Jour de l'An
New Year's Day is the traditional time for the French to exchange such gifts as we Americans give on Christmas, and it is the season when everybody calls on his friends and relatives. It is at New Year's that the old Druidic custom is observed of hanging a large clump of mistletoe above the doorway so that people may exchange kisses when they walk under it.

La Fête des Rois
Just as in English Twelfth Night, the Festival of the Kings is celebrated on Epiphany, January 6th, commemorating the adoration of the Magi. In France it is a family and friendly affair, particularly among religious people. The custom is to meet for dinner and to eat as dessert the *galette des Rois,* a sort of flat cake with a flaky crust in which a bean or small image of the Christ Child has been hidden. The person who gets the bean or image is proclaimed king or queen and must choose a royal partner for the remainder of the evening.

Germany

Christmas was certainly celebrated in Germany as early as the eleventh century, but it was not until the beginning of the twelfth that it passed from mere ecclesiastical and state observance into general and popular feasting. There is a story that Archbishop Adalbert of Bremen, on Christmas Day, 1072, was present at a banquet attended by Duke Magnus and others of his court. After the festive dinner the Duke and guests sang songs which met with the Archbishop's displeasure. He ordered the clerical members of the party to sing clerical songs, but these met with secular displeasure. In anger the Archbishop ordered the table to be lifted, asking God to free him from such captivity. Then he retired, weeping bitterly.

Legend of Luther

One Christmas Eve as Martin Luther was walking across country, he was inspired by the beauty of thousands of stars twinkling in the heavens. When he arrived home, he cut down a fir tree and covered it with small candles so that his children might know what the heavens are like whence Jesus descended to earth. Some historians claim that this was the origin of the Christmas Tree.

Another legend of Christmas Eve tells that there was seen in the forest a miraculous tree in full blossom, covered with candles, and the Christ Child sitting on it. It is said that this scene appeared again centuries later, and the Pope was asked to interpret its meaning. He explained that "the lit tree is humanity; the upright lights are good men; the reversed lights are wicked men; the Child is the Saviour." This story has become part of the popular belief in Germany. The fir trees, bedecked with paper roses, apple and other blossoms, to be found in German houses, are significant of the legendary blossoming of trees on Christmas Eve.

Yet another account is given of the Christmas Tree's origin, that it was a symbol of the winter solstice, which nowadays happens on December 21st-22nd, but many years ago came as late as December 24th, or 25th, or even January 1st or 6th, all depending how many thousands of years you go back. According to this account, the new year begins on the night of December 24th by the sun's turning on its course, and in that moment when the sun stands still, eternity is revealed with all its wonders, and the plant world is endowed with life and blossoming power for another year.

Old Man with the Little Drum

An old German custom is to have an old man, with a little drum attached to his neck and resting on his stomach, lead a procession around the house after the Christmas dinner. The drum major marches into each room to frighten away any witches and to prevent them from returning the following year. Finally the group goes to the children's room, which is opened with great pomp. In the center of the room stands a large Christmas tree, illuminated with candles and laden with gifts for the boys and girls. A huge Janus head or Jack-o'-lantern is placed in the center of the tree, lighted with candles so that flame and smoke issue from its mouth, nose, eyes and ears. Then the children make for the tree and soon strip it of the gifts. The older members of the family also exchange gifts and join in the boisterous play with the children.

Cradle-rocking Songs

Back in 1600 a popular Christmas custom in Germany was "cradle-rocking"; the crib or *krippe* became a cradle, and by rocking the cradle with the image of the Christ Child in it the worshippers expressed their devotion to the newborn Babe. There was much singing and dancing around the cradle, but the stricter members of the Clergy thought it irreverent, so the practice was dropped. Still remain, however, some charmingly simple little cradle-rocking songs addressed to the Christ Child.

ITALY

The Shepherds

A beautiful custom observed for centuries was that of the shepherds coming down from the mountains on Christmas Eve to play pastoral melodies on their bagpipes, in honor of the Holy Child. Their soothing music was more symbolic of the season than the demonstration of any other group.

St. Befana

The good fairy of the Italian children is St. Befana, who at Epiphany rewards children with toys and other presents. Legend has it that she was a woman who was too busy with her housework to offer hospitality to the three Magi Kings and asked them to return when she was not occupied. The three Kings went away and did not come back, so Befana watches for them every Epiphany. Parents threaten to tell Befana when a child is bad, so that she will bring ashes instead of toys. On the Eve of Epiphany a large bowl called the Urn of Fate will be found in most homes; from this urn the children draw some of their gifts.

Spain

The Urn of Fate

Spain also has an Urn of Fate, similar to the one used in Italian homes. For centuries the custom has been to place the names of friends in the bowl; on Christmas Day the names are drawn to decide who shall be devoted friends until next holiday season. The results are sometimes disappointing but everyone grins and bears it.

In the Old Spanish Towns

Before the Civil War, *Noche-Buena* (literally, Good Night) was a time of great activity. The streets were cheerfully lighted and everyone went to the market place for delicious fruits, toys, sweets and other good things to eat. One of the principal entertainments during the Christmas season was the Charity Fair where cards were thrown into a swiftly moving glass jar and lucky numbers were drawn.

In those days, oil lamps were lit in every religious home as soon as the first star appeared on Christmas Eve. On the streets there was gayety until the church bells called to midnight Mass. In every home there is a *Nacimiento* or crib of the Infant Jesus. After breakfast on Christmas morning the children and their parents dance around the *Nacimiento* and sing carols of the Nativity. The holiday in Spain continues until Twelfth Day.

A Spanish Legend

The Wise Men go each year to Bethlehem to pay homage to the Infant Christ. As they pass through Spain they leave gifts of toys and goodies for all well-behaved children. On the Eve of Epiphany the children fill their shoes with straw for the horses of the Wise Men and place them on the windows. In the morning the straw is gone and the shoes are filled with presents. Wealthy citizens of the town distribute the gifts on the window sills of sections where the parents are too poor to buy for the children.

Meeting the Magi

It used to be the custom for the Spanish children to go forth to the city gates to meet the Magi. With joyful hearts they would carry cakes for the Kings, figs for the pages, and hay for the camels. They would visualize the Magi with their blazing torches and gem-set crowns. With the setting of the sun, the vision passed, and the children would wonder which way the Magi went. They would then go home, munching the cakes they brought for the Kings. Later in the evening they would go to church and hear the townsfolk sing, "This morn I met the train of three great Kings of the East."

SWITZERLAND

Rural Customs on Christmas Eve

In many a Swiss peasant home, customs handed down through the centuries are still observed on the night before Christmas. If there is a grandmother in the house, she goes into the basement and selects a perfect onion. She cuts it in half, peels off twelve layers, one for each month of the coming year, and in due rotation she fills each one with salt. The next morning the family can make up a weather forecast for the coming year. The peelings which contain dry salt indicate fair months and the peelings with damp salt presage the rainy months. Mother clips the wings of her chickens before midnight so that they will be safeguarded against all beasts of prey. She is careful, however, not to get within hearing distance of the cattle in the adjoining stable. The cows, the horses and the pigs converse during the hour before midnight of Christmas Eve, and it is unlucky to do any eavesdropping at this time. Father, too, is busy the day before Christmas. It is his job to tie bands of straw around the trunks of the trees in the orchard. This will ensure unusually plentiful crops in the coming year.

Christmas Eve and Cupid

The unmarried youth or girl visits nine different fountains and takes three sips from each, while church bells are calling the faithful to midnight Mass. After completing this curious rite, the future mate will be standing at the church door, and a regular courtship is begun—IF the spell works. After church services the holiday spirit prevails with feasting, dancing, sleigh riding and skiing.

Russia

In the Old Days before the Revolution

Peasants of southern Russia had a custom of welcoming a Christmas guest. A young man, chosen by the villagers for this purpose, would call at the doors of all houses, saying, "Christ is born." The housewife would answer, "In truth He is born," and she would throw some corn on the guest. The young man would then walk to the fire, take up the largest log, and strike until sparks flew. Then he would say, "Even so may blessings come to this house," and place an orange, stuck with a coin, on the end of the log. The housewife would then give him knitted leggings and he would depart with the query, "How did Christmas come to you?" to which the housewife would reply, "As a welcome guest. All have enough and are merry."

In other districts, peasant boys would dress as animals and knock at the doors of houses in the village. They would be invited in and given refreshments and small coins.

For centuries, Christmas ceremonies included the blessing of the river Neva. The river is always frozen over at this season and a little altar was erected on the ice, adorned with pictures of the Saints. A hole was cut in the ice, and in a beautiful and solemn ceremony a cross would be thrown into the water, and priests would bless the river.

The girls in some Russian provinces had a quaint custom of breaking an egg in a glass of water. After watching it take shape, they would place the glass before the shrine of a Saint, and then try to read the future.

Another custom was to put the ring of each guest into a large pan covered with a cloth. Small pieces of charcoal, bread and salt were placed in the pan. The rings were turned with a spoon as the girls sang songs. At the end of each song, a ring was pulled out, and the song that the owner had just sung would foretell her future.

Rumania

Christmas Customs

The shepherds who live in cottages through the valleys and among the hills gather at Christmas time to go from place to place to enact a play which they have given from year to year, and which their ancestors acted before them. It is based on the old story of the Slaughter of the Innocents; the principal characters are Herod, the three Magi, an angel, a child, and two Roman soldiers. Without costume, scenery or props these plain country folk perform in a sincere and impressive fashion.

Young Rumanian girls, anxious to know if they will marry within the next year, enter the stables on New Year's Eve. They strike the foot of the first ox they come across saying, "This year—next year—" If the ox gets up at the first stroke, the girl will marry soon. If the ox gets up at the second stroke, the girl will marry next year. In order to learn the qualities of her future husband, the girl partially disrobes, loosens her hair, bandages her eyes, and braving the cold, goes out into the courtyard and starts to count the stakes in the hedge. She binds the ninth one with ribbon or strands of hair, and returns indoors. The next day she examines the stake. If it is upright and sound, her husband will be young, strong and handsome. If the stake is bent her husband will be old and ugly.

On the *Nosterea Domnului Isus* (Christmas Eve) a special cake called *turta* is eaten. The dough is prepared the night before and is taken into the garden where a tree ceremony takes place to ensure the trees' fruitfulness for the ensuing year. The head of the house threatens to cut down the trees, but the wife prevents him by saying: "Spare this tree for next year and it will be as heavy with fruit as my fingers are with dough."

Epiphany is known in Rumania as *Bobezul Domnului*. At this time the priest goes to the home of his parishioners and blesses them. He dips a bunch of basil in Holy Water and sprinkles the house with it. He carries with him a kettle in which the good people drop coins and gifts of ham, hemp, tongue and some grain. With the hemp, priests are able to make their own cloth, and with the food they are able to support themselves.

Denmark

The Little Yule Dwarf

In Denmark there is no Santa Claus but a *Julenisse*, a little yule gnome or dwarf, thought to dwell in an attic or a barn. He looks after the welfare of the home and brings gifts to the children. He is given a generous portion of *risengrod* (rice pudding) to which an extra lump of butter is added. Horses and cattle are given extra food on Christmas Eve. It is a folk belief that the manger animals stand at midnight in honor of the Christ Child's birth.

Belgium

Goodies to Eat

Belgium has special cakes for the holiday season. They are the flat hard *klaasjes*, the *letterbanket* and the *marsepein*. This last was at one time used in wooing. If a young girl accepted a boy-figure *marsepein* sent by a young man, he knew he had gained his heart's desire. In certain parts of Belgium, if a mist is seen to rise on St. Nicholas' Day (December 6th) the children are told that St. Nicholas is baking his cakes called *zelten*. One story of the origin of the cakes is that three maidens, rescued from shame by St. Nicholas, at their marriage, out of gratitude, baked triple-kneaded rolls and distributed them among poor children.

St. Nicholas' Day

December 6th is St. Nicholas' Day, a day of happiness for the children; for was he not always fond of children? They set up a tree and expect him to make a preliminary visit to their homes the night before. He comes wearing his bishop's robes, his mitre on his head, and his bishop's crozier in his hand. He speaks kindly to good children and promises to return the next morning loaded with gifts. After he leaves, the children hurriedly put out their shoes and place baskets and plates around the room. They also leave hay, carrots, and potato and water for St. Nicholas' horse. When the children arise next morning to find chairs tipped over and the room in confusion, they know that St. Nicholas has been there.

FINLAND

Three Old Customs

Among the Finnish people, Christmas retains some medieval customs. A visit to the bath-house and a change of linen prepares the countryman for Christmas Eve, and early on Christmas morning he drives to church and returns from there at racing speed. The drive back from church has always been an opportunity for showing off the paces of a horse. A pretty custom which used to be universal in the rural districts, but is now very little practiced, was the plaiting of a ceiling or canopy of straw, which was suspended from the rafters; more straw was spread on the floor. This was a reminder of the surroundings in which the Saviour was born. And then, for joy of the season, Christmas games were played on the straw-covered floor. In many parts of the country "star-boys" with blackened faces and quaint costumes go the rounds of the houses, acting the parts of the Wise Men of the East.

Old Man Christmas

On Christmas Eve Old Man Christmas, or as he is also called "The Christmas Goat," arrives from Lapland. He walks in, dressed in a long fur coat and a hoodlike cap, his features invisible behind his white beard and mask or false nose and spectacles. An awe-inspiring sight! The children have been waiting for him for weeks and have written letters to him, and at long last he is here. In a strange wheezy voice he begins to ask questions. Before he will distribute any gifts, he wants to know if the children have been good and obedient. After the presents have been passed out, Old Man Christmas leaves to drive to the next house in his reindeer-drawn sleigh.

A Long Christmas

Christmas is Christmas in Finland, the biggest holiday of the year. It lasts from Christmas Eve through St. Stephen's Day, December 26th. In olden days it lasted right up to Twelfth Night, and even now Twelfth Night is a holiday, not so generally observed as the two and a half days of Christmas, but still a holiday.

Brazil

Papa Noël in the Window

Pape Noël, as Santa Claus is known in Brazil, enters through the window on Christmas Eve, as many of the houses have no chimneys. Gifts are left for the boys and girls in the shoes which they are careful to arrange for his convenience.

An Old Superstition

The legend says that the animals have the power of speech on Christmas night. The children are told that the cock crows in a loud voice at the stroke of twelve, *"Christo nasceu"* (Christ is born). The bull in a deep bass inquires, *"Onde?"* (Where?), and the sheep answer in chorus, *"Em Belem de Juda."* (In Bethlehem of Judea.)

No Christmas Trees in Brazil

The Brazilian child has no Christmas tree, but he has a *presepe* or crèche, representing the Christ Child's birth, with the Holy Family and the shepherds and domestic animals, etc. It is found in private homes as well as in public hospitals and asylums, and is left standing until Epiphany. Gifts and toys are exchanged during the holidays, and then the *presepe* is put away until the following Christmas.

Mexico

The week before Christmas, in Mexico, all cities and towns take on a festival air. Vendors put up booths and stalls displaying handmade carved figures of the Virgin and St. Joseph, the shepherds, and everything in connection with the birth of Christ. In Queretaro, where the ill-fated Emperor Maximilian was executed, allegorical parades take place. No expense is spared in decorating the floats, many of which represent happenings in the New Testament.

In the village of Celaya there is a picturesque custom on Christmas morning. Four sides of the main plaza are taken up by Mexican women, seated on the ground, with baskets in front of them, selling *buñuelos*—a sort of wafer made chiefly of honey. At no other time can these cakes be found there, but hundreds are sold on Christmas Day.

FROM A CHRISTMAS SCRAPBOOK 23

There is a quaint custom among the *pastores* or shepherds. They dress in grotesque clothes, representing anything from an angel to a devil, and go from house to house singing and dancing. The serenaders are usually invited into the home. After the performance, they are treated to refreshments and they are often given small sums of money.

"Merry Christmas" in Many Languages

Brazilian—	*Boas Festas!* (Good Holidays!)
	Feliz Natal! (Happy Christmas!)
Danish—	*Glaedelig Jul!* (Glad Yule!)
Dutch—	*Hartelijke Kerstgroeten!*
English—	*Merry Christmas!*
Finnish—	*Hauskaa Joulua!* (Merry Yule!)
French—	*Joyeux Noël!* (Joyous Christmas!)
German—	*Froehliche Weinachten!*
Italian—	*Bono Natale!* (Good Christmas!)
Portuguese—	*Boas Festas!* (Good Holidays!)
Rumanian—	*Nosteria Lui Christos Sa Va Die de Folos!*
	(May the birth of Christ bring you happiness!)
Spanish—	*¡Felices Pascuas!* (Happy Christmas!)
Swedish—	*God Jul!* (Good Yule!)
Swiss—(French)	*Joyeux Noël!*
(German)	*Froehliche Weinachten!*
(Italian)	*Bono Natale!*

MERRY CHRISTMAS!

CHAPTER III

CHRISTMAS TODAY IN OTHER LANDS

HEAP ANOTHER log on the blazing fire and while it crackles with contentment, we will take an armchair cruise to distant lands across the sea. In radio style let's make a holiday hookup and tune in our friends and relatives in Merrie England, in France, in Germany, in Italy, in Denmark and other countries where the spirit of Christmas still lives.

Join us, young and old, one and all, in this visit to where our cousins are gathered in their homes for a single purpose: to commemorate the birth of Him whose teachings we must follow if ultimately we are to have "Peace on Earth, Good Will Toward Men."

Our nation-to-nation broadcast carries us first to the voice of our English cousin, Cyril Blackstone, who tells us about

CHRISTMAS IN MERRIE ENGLAND
"Cheerio! We are celebrating Christmas in pretty much the same way as you are in America. Generosity on a broad scale is only equalled by joviality everywhere. An infectious spirit permeates the city streets and village lanes, with care and trouble banished from sight. Yes, an English Christmas is the same, with the exchange of presents an outstanding feature. Then, too, there is the singing of Christmas carols on the highways as well as in the churches throughout the land.

"December 26th, the day after Christmas, is known as Boxing Day and is observed on a scale almost equal to that of Christmas Day. Boxing Day was originally the time for the village priest to open the poor box in the parish house and distribute the money. Nowadays, mail-carriers, newsboys and other public servants ask for Christmas gifts on Boxing Day, as they make their rounds from house to house. The visitor extends the season's greetings and awaits in eager anticipation until you give him a shilling or two, a custom which seems to be mutually understood.

"If you happen in London Christmas Eve, by all means attend the carol recitals in Westminster Abbey, St. Paul's Cathedral or the Temple Church. It is an inspiring experience and one which you will never forget. In London as well as the seaside cities the hotels are now doing a great deal to keep the tradition of a merry Christmas and to make their guests really feel at home.

"I have been asked, 'What about that famous ritual of the feast, the bringing in of the boar's head?' It isn't done any more except at Queen's College and at some of the leading hotels in London and nearby points. At Queen's a boar's head is always bedecked with bay leaves and rosemary and placed on the banquet boards as a prelude to the sumptuous Christmas dinner.

"In a few country estates Christmas is celebrated in the good old-fashioned way. There is, for instance, the ancient practice of burning the Yule Log and laying aside one-half of the consumed log until next year. Tradition states that this will preserve the house from the danger of fire.

"Another rural custom still in vogue is the ceremony of the farmer and his friends who drink a toast of cider to the favorite apple tree.

"Then, too, the Christmas Mummers are still in existence, with the same plays which have been presented for the past several hundred years. These traditional affairs are observed in Gloucestershire, Oxfordshire, Hampshire and Warwickshire. At Stratford-on-Avon the Christmas Mummers perform just as they acted over three hundred and fifty years ago when William Shakespeare was an interested spectator. If you visit England at Christmas be sure to see this spectacle and if possible, stay until Boxing Day for the meet of the foxhounds in this Warwickshire village where the Immortal Bard was born.

"On one point about Christmas in England I must disillusion you. If you are visualizing a blanket of white snow over the countryside such as Dickens describes in his books, or such as you see pictured on greeting cards, you are doomed to disappointment.

There hasn't been old-fashioned holiday weather here for many years!"

The next message is from Paris and Pierre Arnaud is our composite voice:

FRANCE

"Christmas in France is limited to a distribution of gifts among the children and to boisterous Christmas Eve celebrations in the larger cities where the midnight supper takes the place of the usual dinner next day. It is true that there are religious ceremonies in the Church just as there are in other Christian nations, but to the French the universal exchange of presents is made on New Year's Day.

"The first of the year is the time of the greatest festival and is to the native of France what Christmas is in America, the giving and receiving of gifts. This is the great family day and the most cherished of all red-letter days on the calendar. The children come in for another round of presents from St. Nicholas and delightful things are given not only to cousins, aunts and uncles, beside the immediate family, but also to the servants and the tradesmen who have served the family the past year.

"Paris and other large cities are brightly decorated and noisy crowds fill the streets shouting greetings to one another.

"The greeting-card custom is more extensive in France at New Year's than it is in other countries at Christmas. On this occasion it is almost a duty to mail greetings to every acquaintance one can recall to mind. In fact, the average person will feel neglected if he does not receive at least a hundred cards.

"After the dinner has been enjoyed with the immediate family, the younger members assemble at the home of the oldest for an evening feast. This is, in fact, a home-coming with relatives from far and near gathering for the purpose of dining and saluting the newborn year with many hours of fun making in which all take part."

GERMANY

Come in, "Konrad Hahn," and tell us something about Christmas in Germany:

"Wie Gehts! In this land where many Christmas traditions began, the holiday extends over a period of three days. By unanimous consent all kinds of work are suspended the day before the holiday and activity is not resumed until the day after. When dusk falls on the night before Christmas, the streets are emptied and there is a general gathering around the family tree. Almost every home has a brilliantly decorated tree with presents for all on a nearby table. Gifts are exchanged, the family makes merry and good cheer prevails until a late hour.

"In Germany toy giving is inseparably connected with this great feast of the year. Indeed, the toy is the eternal wand by which to conjure upon the Land of Heart's Desire. Toy-making is a great industry in Germany. The districts which are the centers of this ancient folk art are old farming country. This is why the majority of German toys reflect the objects of the old farmsteads: house and stable, cows and horses, drivers and carts, woods and wild game. The German toy area is still located for the most part in the Great Forest districts, and even though modern methods are now behind these activities, the makers still retain the old simplicity of design which has always been characteristic of the present-made toy. If one visits the toy makers of Thuringia, in the Erz Gebirge, or in Bavaria, one immediately senses this pleasant note.

"The lovely custom of the Christmas market in old Nuremberg or in the front of the medieval Römerberg in Frankfort is a happy throw-back into the land of childhood and the past. Even the Berlin Lustgarten, which is otherwise framed by the austere façade of the Palace, the Cathedral and the old Museum, becomes astonishingly bewitched. Here in the snow-covered alleys between the booths, in the midst of nutcrackers, the jumping jacks and incense burners, are spread out gingerbread men, gay toys and bright Christmas-tree ornaments. The loud calls of the hawkers in praise of their wonderful wares mix with the laughter of the buyers and onlookers, the shrieking of toy trumpets and the whistling screech of the *Waldteufel* made of pasteboard.

"From the happy hearts of the children, who in the joy of toys are all equal, be they poor or rich, a spark goes out to the grownups because it is Christmastide and the bells are pealing 'Peace on Earth.'"

In Sunny Italy

Thank you, Herr Hahn. And now, here we are in Italy and stepping up to the microphone is Antonio Crosetti, who speaks to us from Rome:

"Christmas in Italy is more of a festival for grownups than for children. Families gather together on Christmas Eve and talk around the fireplace while they watch the *appo*, the Christmas log throwing its sparks up the chimney. Then they sit down to supper, the *cenone*, at which there is no meat (for Christmas Eve is a fast day) but interminable dishes prepared in every way imaginable, and *pangiallo*—yellow bread—of corn flour with raisins. For sweetmeats, there is *torrone*, a hard candy made of almonds and honey. The meal ends just before twelve when all go to midnight Mass.

"A kindly old lady called Befana is in the minds of the Italian boys and girls as the Christmas season draws near. For there is no Santa Claus here—snow and reindeer, the scarlet-clad one and his white beard belong to the Hyperboreans who cluster around the North Pole, at least in the thoughts of the peoples inhabiting the sun-bathed lands of the Mediterranean.

"The little Italian expects his gifts not on Christmas Day, but at Epiphany, January 6th. This is perhaps more logical, for Epiphany commemorates the three Magi who came to the manger in Bethlehem bearing presents of gold, frankincense and myrrh.

"Befana, the good-natured old lady, flies in through the window, which is left open, and puts her presents near a manger which the optimistic children have rigged up. For bad children, and this preserves household tranquillity for a month before Epiphany—Befana brings only charcoal!"

Introducing Alexis Krivochev, who will tell us about Christmas customs.

In Old Russia

"When I was a child, in my native land there was always a pre-Christmas fast beginning on the 15th and ending on the 24th. At sunset, when the first star appeared in the sky, the villagers sat down to their evening meal consisting chiefly of fish, topped with a dessert called *contia*. There are several kinds of *contia;* it may be boiled rice with jam, or boiled wheat with honey, or a large but very thin, dry and sweet cracker. This is broken into small pieces and covered with poppy seed.

"At night we sang Christmas carols and trimmed the tree, decorated the way it is here in America. There was no Santa Claus in Russia. True, there was a slight similarity between Santa Claus and Grandfather Frost, but no one believed he made any toys. The children knew, always, that the toys came from their parents. On Christmas the families held happy reunions with parties for the children."

Now, we will look to H. Ramo for an account of

CHRISTMAS IN FINLAND

"In the Finnish home the Christmas tree (always a fir tree) is set up on Christmas Eve. Apples and other fruits, candies, paper flags, cotton and tinsel are used to decorate the tree, and candles are always used for lighting it.

"The Christmas festivities are always preceded by a visit to the *sauna*, the famous Finnish steambath, after which everyone dresses in clean clothes in preparation for the Christmas dinner, which is served anywhere from 5 to 7 P.M.

"Christmas gifts may be given out before or after the dinner, depending on the family. The children do not hang up stockings, but Santa Claus comes in himself, often accompanied by as many as half a dozen Christmas elves (in brown costumes, knee-length pants, red stockings, red elves' caps), to distribute the presents.

"The main dish of the dinner is boiled codfish, served snowy white and fluffy, with allspice, boiled potatoes and cream sauce. The dried cod has been soaked for a week in a lye solution, then in clear water, to soften it to the right texture.

"Also on the menu will be found a roast suckling pig or a roast fresh ham, *puolukka* jam, mashed potatoes and vegetables. Finnish bakeries make a special Christmas bread of rye seasoned with molasses. There will also be homemade black bread, *kovaa leipää* or hardtack, *nisua* or coffee cake, *korppua* or toasted coffee cake.

"After dinner the children go to bed, their elders staying up to chat with visitors and drink coffee until about midnight, when everybody retires in order to get up early next morning for church.

"Christmas Day services in the churches begin at 6 A.M. After church the families come back home, or go to their relatives for dinner. Christmas Day is very quiet—a day of family visits and reunions. In some parts of the country the *Tähti Pojat*, Star-Boys, tour the countryside singing Christmas songs.

"The Christmas festivities continue for two more days. December 26th is *Tapanin Päivä* or St. Stephen's Day, one of the features of which, especially in the country, is the traditional *Tapanin Ajo* —a drive through the country roads racing the best horses. *Tapanin Päivä* is a much more festive day and the evening is usually spent in dancing.

"December 27th, the festivities and visits continue. On all these days people keep wishing each other *'Hauskaa Joulua!'* (Merry Yule!)."

Twist the dial again and you will hear Wilhelm Eickhoff give a short but interesting account of the Christmas celebration in

Denmark

"In Denmark, as in all Scandinavian and other European countries, Christmas is celebrated on Christmas Eve, December 24th. At five o'clock it is customary to go to church, and all over the city the church bells are heard chiming. The beautiful Danish Christmas carols are sung not only by the choir but by the whole congregation.

"A real Danish Christmas dinner consists of rice-porridge, roast goose stuffed with prunes and apples, served with vegetables, such as potatoes and red cabbage and as dessert, Danish apple cake with whipped cream. When the rice-porridge is being served, an almond (blanched) is hidden in one of the portions, and the one who happens to get the almond is entitled to an extra Christmas gift called 'the almond gift.'

"For the children the most exciting moment is when the door is swung open and the Christmas tree (always spruce, never pine) is seen in all its beauty, decorated from top to bottom and with the gifts hidden under the tree. Little Danish children do not know the custom of hanging the Christmas stockings.

"First and second Christmas days are church holidays also.

"Nobody must be forgotten during Christmas so all the poor and sick are well taken care of with food and toys, and in all the hospitals the nurses have decorated the rooms with evergreens and many other things, and in the halls huge Christmas trees are put up.

"In the country the farmer is very careful that all the cattle, pigs, chickens and so on have an extra good ration of feed. There are in Denmark quite a few superstitious tales about Christmas, one is that no farmer must forget to make a cross in front of the entrance that no evil will cross his threshold during the holidays—and he has to remember to put a big portion of rice-porridge out in the barn for all the small brownies.

"It is a custom to bake plenty of different cookies before Christmas, and there is an old saying that if you call on somebody and eat nothing, you carry Christmas away from the home."

Let's glide to a land where scenic beauty blends with sincere hospitality to make the season most delightful for foreign winter guests as well as the natives. Here is Herr Dossenbach, with his message,

CHRISTMAS IN SWITZERLAND

"This is Christmas Land indeed, with everything glistening in the pure white snow, the air perfumed by the stately pine trees and sleigh bells singing merry melodies as the horses briskly travel over the mountain roads.

"Old St. Nicholas has been succeeded in many parts of Switzerland by the Christkindli (Christ Child), an angelic figure who travels over the land every Christmas Eve in a beautiful sleigh drawn by six reindeer. The sleigh is heavily laden with Christmas trees, fruit, cookies and toys for the children.

"In every home there is a Christmas tree about which the family gathers and sings carols while the youngsters enjoy their new playthings. In thousands of these homes, the head of the family opens the big Bible and reads St. Luke's account of the birth of Christ.

"In the country districts, Santa Claus remains a great favorite with the children. He does not make his visit on Christmas Eve but on December 6th, the anniversary of the first St. Nicholas who had the custom of giving secret presents to the poor, and was especially kind to children. He lived in Asia Minor where he ruled as Bishop in the fourth century.

"In some rural communities the boys of school age arrange a parade with Santa Claus at the head of the procession. The march-

CHRISTMAS TODAY IN OTHER LANDS 33

ers stop at various homes to collect small gifts, and even go to neighboring towns for donations. In the evening they assemble at the town hall where the gifts are equally divided.

"Santa Claus is also honored with impressive ceremonies on December 6th at Zurich where a giant St. Nicholas leads a parade of young admirers dressed in long white nightgowns and wearing grotesque masks and headgear. The boys make merry with horns and bells as they solicit gifts of toys and fruit from the spectators along the route of the parade."

Let us transfer our program at this time, while Nicolade Bibescu sends greetings from

RUMANIA

"Merry Christmas! Here in Rumania this Christian holiday is also a time for celebration according to superstition and tradition entirely foreign to the Orthodox faith. This is especially true in the rural sections where peasants have their own idea of holidays. While the rites lean toward paganism, they are known by the saint days of the Gregorian calendar.

"The 22nd of December, for example, (St. Ignatius Day in the Eastern Church) is popularly called 'Ignat' and is the time when the pig is killed and dressed for the Christmas feast.

"A touch of Dionysus worship is manifested in *Brezaia*, a celebration held on the day before Christmas. At this time young men and boys dance in the streets with effigies in the shape of a goat's head on a long pole and with a string attached to the mouth so that it may be manipulated like a ventriloquist's dummy.

"A play known as *Irozii*, depicting the birth of Christ and the flight into Egypt, is produced continually from Christmas Day to Epiphany. On New Year's Day, the male youths march in the streets with an ox-drawn plow. The way is cleared by two young men ringing a large bell while the others follow the plow to the accompaniment of cracking whips and bagpipe music."

And now, if you will spin the indicator a bit to the left, you will hear a friendly voice speaking to you from Brussels, the capital of

BELGIUM

"Here the Christmas spirit prevails the same as in other Christian countries but the day is celebrated in a manner somewhat different from that in the United States.

"In Belgium, Christmas Day is marked chiefly by religious services in the churches, by family gatherings, and by visits among friends.

"A few families now have a Christmas tree, as you have in America, but that is not a general custom throughout the country. Nor is it the Belgium custom to give presents to children on that day as it is in America. However, the boys and girls are not forgotten during the Holy Season. Santa Claus brings them gifts on December 6th, which is St. Nicholas Day in the Church calendar. On the eve of that day, the Belgian children place their shoes by the chimney hearth, instead of hanging up their stockings on Christmas Eve, as is done in the United States.

"The great majority of Belgians are of Catholic faith and are noted for their deep religious feeling. Christmas is to them a specially joyous feast day because of its religious significance. There are special religious services and the *Crèche* is set up in the Catholic churches, as is also done in other countries.

"On Christmas Eve, services are held in the churches and midnight Mass is celebrated. Christmas carols (called '*Noëls*') are also sung on that night to usher in the day of our Lord's Nativity. There are many such Christmas carols, some of them dating from the Middle Ages while others are of modern origin. One of the favorite carols, sung at midnight on Christmas Eve, begins as follows:

> *Minuit, Chrétiens, c'est l'heure solenelle*
> *Où Homme-Dieu descendit jusq'à nous*
> *Pour effacer la tâche originelle*
> *Et de Son Père arrêter le courroux.*

"An English version of this carol, composed by Adolphe Adam (1803-1856), is used in American churches, sung to the same solemn and inspiring music."

In Latin America, existing Christmas customs have been inherited from those who first brought them from the home land across the sea. Thus, in states and countries where the majority of the residents are Italian, Portuguese, German or Spanish, the religious festivals and celebrations continue the pre-war custom in the country of their forefathers.

We are indebted to Andrés Pastorize for this Christmas Day information from the

Dominican Republic

"In my country, Christmas is a religious holiday more than anything else, and the traditional Christmas dinner is held on the 24th, generally after midnight Mass. Christmas carols are sung in the streets, and are called '*aguinaldos.*'

"Although the increasing trade and social relations with the United States have popularized Santa Claus, children still receive their presents on the sixth of January, when the three Wise Men of the Orient paid their visit to the Holy Child and brought him offerings of myrrh, frankincense and gold.

"The New Year is always joyously acclaimed with social, familiar and popular rejoicings."

The next speaker will be Mario Guimaraes, who will enlighten us on Christmas customs in

Brazil

"In Brazil, Christmas is celebrated very much as it is here in the United States, although in our language Santa Claus is called *Papa Noël*. He is dressed like your Santa Claus and he comes with his reindeer and sleigh even though we are in the southern hemisphere where Christmas is in the summer time. We have cold weather in winter only in our southern States, and yet we cling to the old traditions handed down to us by our forefathers who came from Portugal and other European countries.

"At eleven o'clock on Christmas Eve the churches celebrate the *Missa do Gallo*. This mass is one of the most impressive and stirring of the whole year. It is followed by the singing of Christmas carols.

"After the mass, it is customary to have a family supper or *consoada,* in the home, and, even though the hour is late, these suppers are very popular. All members of the family are expected, and they visit and sing carols just as you do at your family parties.

"We also have the custom of the hanging of stockings, but we put out the shoes also. They are usually put in the kitchen, which at first thought seems strange; but when you remember that the custom arose in the northern countries where Christmas is in the winter time and the tradition is that Santa Claus comes down the chimney, it is only natural that we put ours near the kitchen stove—the only heat used in the summer time. Some very poor people put their shoes on the roof, as being more convenient for *Papa Noël*.

"Another heritage from European customs is the *presepe*, or representation of the Christ child lying in a manger, which is believed to have been originated by St. Francis of Assisi in 1223. These are prepared in the churches and in the homes, and some of them are very elaborate, representing the stable and its surroundings, together with members of the Holy Family and other scriptural characters, both human and animal. The *presepe* is arranged just before Christmas and is kept until January 6th, the 'Day of Kings,' or 'Little Christmas,' as it is sometimes called in this country.

" 'The Day of Kings' commemorates the visit to the Christ Child of the Wise Men from the East. Inasmuch as they came on camels, Brazilian children look forward to the coming of the 'King' on his camel, bringing them toys and other gifts. In turn, they put out a little offering of corn for the poor tired beast.

"You will see, therefore, that in Brazil Christmas festivities begin on December 24th and continue until January 6th."

To Señor Rafael Fuentes we are grateful for these details regarding Christmas festivities in

MEXICO

"A pretty custom peculiar to Mexico is the use of a *piñata*. This is a clay bowl elaborately decorated with tissue paper of different colors, and taking the shape sometimes of an animal, sometimes of a bird, an airplane, a '*charro*'—the national native Mexican type —or simply something just to give it an outside colorful appearance. The bowl is filled with fresh fruit of the season, also peanuts and candy. The *piñata* is hung in the middle of the patio and usually children, but adults, sometimes, too, try to break the clay bowl with a stick releasing the fruit, and all attending the party go on the floor to pick up some of the fruit. The one who tries to break the *piñata* is blindfolded and he is given several chances, after which another guest takes his place.

"It is also customary in Mexico to have nine continuous days of what is called *posadas*, which are nine parties, one on each night preceding Christmas. People usually dance at those parties and are given by the host a small present; it may be in porcelain, with candy inside, or simply small candy packages wrapped in crepe paper.

"Mexicans have their Christmas dinner on Christmas Eve and not on Christmas Day, usually after ten o'clock at night."

And finally, we have reached the country where Christmas is observed in a big way. In fact, the season continues for an entire month! Through the courtesy of Anne Stoddard, editor of the *American Girl*, we bring you this message from Fairfax Downey about

SWEDEN

"Twelve days before Christmas the Swedish Christmas begins with the tradition of Lucia, a beautiful Christian maiden who lived in Rome. When she refused to give up her religion and marry a pagan, she was burned at the stake during the persecutions by the Emperor Diocletian. The story of her martyrdom and sainthood was carried North to Scandinavia by the missionaries. To the brave Viking people, accepting Christianity, St. Lucia appealed strongly. Since her saint's day happened to fall on December 13th, about the time when daylight begins to increase, she became even more of a favorite with the Northerners. The ancient custom of presenting Lucia, first in church Christmas pageants, is now carried out in the homes. Because some homes do not have a daughter to take the part, a Lucia Queen has been elected by popular vote.

"From this charming beginning, the Swedish Christmas continues until January 13th during which time many other traditions are celebrated. There is, for example, December 22nd, the day for bringing in Christmas trees. Every home has a tree which is set up in the living room and colorfully decorated. The presents are wrapped and placed under the tree, to be opened on Christmas Eve. This is the evening for family reunions with plenty of good things to eat. While the tree and presents are being admired, there enters, not Santa Claus, but the Gnome of Good Luck. His arms are piled high with more presents, which he leaves on the floor, and quickly departs. The packages are opened and then all join hands, first circling the tree and then parading through the house singing merry Yuletide tunes. Festivities continue until January 13th when Christmas comes to an official end with parties and smaller gatherings in the homes."

CHAPTER IV

THE CHRISTMAS PARTY

HOLIDAY GATHERINGS that are remembered pleasantly are usually the result of careful planning. Whether you are playing host to eight or to eighty people, the same care must be exercised. For the club leader, the teacher, the members of any entertainment or program committee, this chapter offers many helpful suggestions as to the decorations, describes games to be played, and gives recipes for the refreshments to be served. In another chapter you will find the poems and stories appropriate for recitations and for reading aloud. And you will want to make generous use of the Christmas carols, which start on page 87.

A good leader must become thoroughly familiar with the games planned, at least a day before the date of the party or social. The secret of a popular Christmas party is to start off by getting everybody well acquainted at the very beginning. Creating this really social atmosphere from the moment the guests arrive is the first problem facing the leader. The next task is to balance the activities so that there will not be too many pencil and paper games, too many team contests, or too much action among the few with the others not participating. In case the program of games you have outlined does not click the way you expected, always have an alternate list of stunts on hand so that you can make a last-minute switch.

It is better to have too many games on hand than not enough. For this reason, select a few extra numbers to take care of any miscalculation you might make in time. Finally, the leader must thoroughly understand the games and manifest genuine enthusiasm in them as the directions are given to others. Another thing, change the game while it is at the height of its popularity. Don't wait until interest sags, and, if you can end the party on a high pitch, before the group is tired and anxious to leave, you will be a popular and successful hostess.

For suggested outlines of parties, see pages 42 and 56.

THE HOME-COMING PARTY

When relatives gather from far and near, it is presumed they are well enough acquainted to dispense with the usual warming-up stunts, such as are described below as "Ice Breakers." However, this is not always the case nowadays. Since last reunion, Grandmother's oldest son from five hundred miles away has become a father-in-law, and two daughters of another son have taken unto themselves nice, new shiny husbands. One son is bringing the "girl of his dreams." The family group, too, is often augmented by old friends who have no families of their own with whom they might spend Christmas. They are always welcomed at this joyous season, and made to feel comfortably at home.

There is no method more direct than all-around introductions and the exchange of the holiday greeting, "Merry Christmas!" at the home-coming affair. Following this, the program is usually one which has been carried out the same, year after year. The writer knows of one family party which starts early Christmas afternoon when the group assembles in a brightly decorated room, with Grandfather on one side of the crackling fireplace and an expansive Christmas tree on the other. Under the tree, huge baskets of gifts have been stacked, to be distributed by the head of the house. This is the first thing on the schedule. With everyone tense, and all anxiously awaiting their presents, Grandfather adjusts his spectacles and assumes his annual rôle of Santa Claus. He calls out the name of the recipient, who steps forward to get the package. One by one the names are called until all the bundles have been passed out. The gifts include those which the family members exchange with each other, and Grandmother makes sure that friends of the family also receive something. The packages are not opened until all have been allocated. Then, Grandfather gives the signal and the paper begins to fly. After the gifts have been admired individually and collectively, the paper, string, boxes and other containers are taken into the cellar, and the room is cleared for action.

THE CHRISTMAS PARTY 43

Various games are introduced each year. This coming Christmas the program will start with the singing of carols in relays. One member of the circle will start the carol, singing just one line, as "Hark! The herald angels sing"; the next person to the right will sing the second line, "Glory to the newborn King." The person to his right will then sing the third line, and so on until the piece is finished. After singing two or three carols in this manner, the following games, taken from this book, will be played:

> Christmas Pantomime (page 45)
> Christmas Word Game (page 46)
> Christmas Scents (page 47)
> Christmas Bee (page 48)
> Bubble-Blowing Contest (page 51)

There will be an intermission of singing Christmas carols, to be followed by the quizzes arranged at the end of this chapter.

The greatest event of the day, Grandmother's Christmas Dinner, will then be served, followed by an evening around the fireplace, telling stories, singing carols, and listening to the younger members recite Yuletide poems of long standing.

GAMES

Ice Breakers

Christmas Animals

This game is guaranteed to thaw that reserve which so often freezes conversation at the beginning of a party. There will be no embarrassing Arctic silences after the Christmas animals have had their say!

Have a card ready for each person. At the top of the blank card write the name of an animal. Each name is to be duplicated, one card being given to the young woman and one to the young man. After the cards have been distributed a signal is given, and one elephant must hunt through the crowd for the other elephant, one monkey for the other monkey, one lion for the other lion, etc. When the "animals" have been paired, each couple draws a little apart from the crowd and together they compose two telegrams, the words of which must begin with the letters composing the animal's name, in their correct order. The girl's telegram must be addressed to the man and his must be a reply to it. Five or six minutes are allowed for this effort, after which the telegrams are handed to the hostess. She reads them aloud and the audience chooses the best telegram and its answer.

Heil Holiday!

Have the guests stand around the hall. The leader turns to his right, and walks around the inside of the circle, pinching lightly the cheek of each guest and saying, "Merry Christmas!" giving his name and receiving his or her name in return. The first person saluted will follow closely behind the leader, doing the same; the second follows—and so on. Soon the circle will be turning in on itself, and a long line will be following the leader. No one moves until his neighbor at the left has himself turned inward and joined the face-pinching procession. The player on the left of the leader, at the beginning of the procedure, is the only one who does not move. When the rite is finished, everyone will have spoken to everyone else and will feel better acquainted through the cheek-pinching salute.

Christmas "If" Scavenger Hunt

Cut as many paper arrows as you wish to use. On each paper arrow write directions similar to the suggestions given below. Each paper arrow has a number, i.e., from No. 1 to say No. 7, or whatever number you wish to place around the house. (Pin on curtains, put under a lamp base so that only a small piece shows, etc.) Caution your guests that they must follow the arrows consecutively. The directions on the last arrow should bring the players all together, as in No. 7 below.

Examples:

1. If you are wearing any green go to the kitchen, get a dish from the cupboard, wash and dry it and put it away.

2. If you use torrid adjectives while hunting for a collar button, say "Oh, Fishhooks, excuse me," five times to anyone who will listen.

3. If you ever quarrel with your mate, go and kiss him or her.

4. If your hair is curly, put some water on the front lock until it is straight.

5. If you ever oversleep in the morning, find an alarm clock and set it so that it will ring within fifteen minutes.

6. If you ever baked a cake that "fell," sit down on the floor and cry.

7. If you brush your teeth daily, go sit down in the living room but don't smile or speak until your host or hostess appears.

Christmas Pantomime

Write the names of your guests on slips of paper. Place the names of the women in one bowl and the names of the men in the other. Pass the first bowl among the men or the bowl with the men's names among the women. Each takes a name and finds his or her partner. Now, pass another receptacle around to everyone. In this bowl you will have written on as many slips as needed, various subjects to be portrayed by each couple, completely by pantomime. Here are listed a few suggestions:

1. A man buying his wife a Christmas present.
2. A man and woman trimming a Christmas tree.
3. A man and woman trying to wrap a large package with a small piece of paper.
4. A woman buying a Christmas tree.
5. A man and woman singing a Christmas carol.
6. A husband putting up Christmas decorations under his wife's supervision.

Tree Auction

You will undoubtedly have among the party members a man or woman with a store of wit and humor who can successfully act as an auctioneer. The auctioneer has one tree left which he must dispose of. The rest of the party are potential purchasers. With a gift for repartee, the auctioneer soon has the others entering into the spirit of the occasion and many of the bidders will probably contribute equally amusing (and probably disparaging) remarks about the tree.

Contrary Christmas Challengers

Seat the members of the party opposite each other. The host or hostess may act as "Leader." It is the duty of the leader to give each person a task. Instead of doing what he is asked, however, the player does exactly the opposite. Here are a few pointers to start you off:

1. Stand on your head and do not recite a Christmas jingle.
2. Put your right hand on your hip and smile but do not say, "A merry Christmas to all and to all a good night!"
3. Do not chew a cud as a cow chews and do not wish all a Happy New Year for many moons to come.
4. Raise the window shade with your right hand. (Should be raised with left hand.)
5. Smile and chew a Christmas cookie on the left side of your mouth.
6. Take a ball from the top of the tree and put it on the bottom. (Should be taken from the bottom and placed at the top.)
7. Spell Merry Christmas. (Should be spelled samtsirhC yrreM)
8. Walk to the light switch and turn off the light. (Player should walk to the kitchen and turn on the light.)
9. Take a pencil and draw a cartoon of the person sitting at your right. (Should be person sitting at left.)
10. Do not say, "Certain cinnamon Christmas cookies created conscientiously clearly cause children to cater constantly." (You'd better write this out.)

Pencil and Pad Pastimes

Christmas Word Game

After distributing pencils and pads to each guest, announce that the best prize of the evening will be awarded to the contestant who can form the most words out of the phrase, "Merry Christmas to You." Explain that letters used in forming one word may be used again in making another word. The game continues for five minutes, when papers are collected. The player with the greatest number of true and correct words is immediately awarded the grand prize of the evening. A "booby" prize in the form of a ten-cent dictionary may be presented to the player having the *least* number of words.

Christmas Scents
If you have any sense of differentiating scents, now is the time to use them. Distribute among the guests sheets of paper, each sheet being numbered from one to ten. Before the arrival of your guests prepare a tray containing bags of various things of distinct aroma. Pass the tray around so that every player will have an opportunity to test his olfactory nerves. Each of the bags to be sniffed should be marked with a number. The players write down the names of the contents according to the smell. Here are suggested articles to place in the bags: 1, Pine needles; 2, Cedar shavings; 3, Coffee; 4, Tea; 5, Cheese; 6, Piece of apple; 7, Orange skin; 8, Peppermint candy; 9, Spices; 10, Onion.

Christmas Toy Shopping
"Get your pencils and pads ready, Everybody! We are going to tour the Merchant Department Store with our holiday list." With this explanation the hostess proceeds to assign to each guest one of the following problems which he is to answer by listing as many toys as he can remember which might be suitable.

1. For a boy of seven who is mechanically inclined.
2. For a father who gets a kick out of his children's toys.
3. For a practical joker.
4. For a young girl who is athletically inclined.
5. For a serious-minded child of 12.
6. For a girl of 13 who likes to draw.
7. For a boy of 14 who wants to become a writer.

This list will give you an idea of the kind of questions to ask. If you wish to make it more personal and perhaps more humorous, you might suggest that toys be bought for various members of the party. Allow five or six minutes for the answers.

Christmas Cablegrams
As soon as pencils and pads have been distributed, the leader selects a word and announces it. The players attempt to make up

a cablegram, beginning each word of the message with one of the letters of the announced word, in consecutive order.

Four minutes are allowed and the player having the best sentence wins. Here is an example: The word chosen is "MERRY" and the resulting cablegram: "Mary East Righteously Rejects Yachting." Or, it might be: "May Every Riotous Reveler Yell."

Christmas Bee

You begin this pencil-and-pad pastime by selecting a letter. If you decide upon "B," tell the players to write as many popular gifts as they can think of beginning with that letter: Bible, ball, bat, belt, beads, bag, brush, boat, baby, bell, bicycle, Buick, book, basket, and so on. Three minutes may be allotted for writing. The game may be continued with different letters as long as the group evinces interest.

The Life of the Party

Christmas Concert

Choose a well-known Christmas carol for your concert. See chapter beginning on page 87. If the hostess does not play the piano, then ask for a volunteer pianist. The rest of the musicians are to follow the accompaniment of the piano with various homemade instruments. This is a game in which everyone can participate and will create a great deal of merriment. Here are a few pointers in case you need a little assistance for the homemade instruments.

Improvised musical instruments for the concert: A piece of wood or tough cardboard over which is stretched a rubber band; a thin silver spoon and lightweight tumbler.

Dickens' "Christmas Carol" Quiz

Have someone read several pages in the first chapter of *A Christmas Carol*—about the first ten pages would be enough, although the listeners will probably enjoy more. Give each member of the audience a pencil and sheet of paper. As the story is read, the listeners are to jot down any well-known phrase or bit of philosophy that is suggested, as the simile, "dead as a door-nail" or the phrase "good for anything he chose to put his hand to"— you will find everyday slang as "cut up" (Scrooge, you remember,

THE CHRISTMAS PARTY 49

was not dreadfully "cut up" over Marley's death). Literary references noted may also be used in the list (reference to Shakespeare's *Hamlet*)—even the mention of a well-known place should be acceptable, as St. Paul's Churchyard, for you must remember this game will require concentration and a bit of quick thinking on the part of your guests.

Easy Christmas Poetry
Ask your guests as a group the following lines of *Santa's Adventures*. They must answer with a word or phrase that rhymes with the last word of the statement.

1. "The doors were locked, the windows shut, alas there was no chimney."
A. "There was naught to do but use his key."
or "He could not climb a tree."
or "Poor Santa's up a tree."
or "And he couldn't write poetry."

The answering jingle does not have to make sense, in fact the more ridiculous, the better. Now then, read the second line which is:

2. "He had so many trips to make, that this delay was worry real," and wait for the next guest-poet's inspiration.
A. "Ruth must have her doll, and Tom his rod and reel."
3. "But once the good old boy got in some way,"
A. "The toys and goodies did leave his pack without delay."
4. "Then, on to the next snow-covered waiting home"
A. "Rushed dear old Santa, loved o'er sea and foam"
5. "Gifts for all—the good I mean—coal for the naughty"
A. "Neckties for Dad, a rattle for baby, and for Mama a Scotty"
6. "Sad yet happy now his work is over, a sigh he breathes,"
A. "All done my fun till next year's come, as he homeward weaves."

Concealed Christmas Seals
Purchase two packages of assorted Christmas Seals. Save one package for your prize. Take one package and remove the seals, then place them around the recreation rooms in inconspicuous

places—in designs of rugs, on pictures, on curtains, under sides of tables and chairs, etc. Tell your guests that the room is full of concealed Chrristmas Greetings, and the one who finds the greatest number of them is to receive a prize worthy of his efforts. Remember to paste the seals lightly at one tip only, so that they can be easily removed.

Trimming the Christmas Tree

Have the players sit in a circle, with one in the middle who says, "I have a Christmas tree. What will you give me to put on it?" The player at the beginning of the circle starts with something beginning with the first letter of the alphabet, A, for instance, an Ark, or Amber lights. The next answers with the letter B, e.g., Balloons or Bulbs. The third will give an article beginning with C, for instance, Candy or Candles. This continues until the entire alphabet has been used. The answers must follow quickly after one another so that the game will not drag. Should a player hesitate he loses a "life." He is out of the game after the loss of two "lives."

Curving Christmas Cards

Place a wastebasket in the center of the group and have the players toss six of last year's Christmas cards, one at a time, into the receptacle. There is a lot of "curve" to a card flung only a few feet away and one must employ plenty of skill to toss them into the basket.

After five rounds or innings, the one who has succeeded in throwing the greatest number of Christmas cards into the container is declared the winner.

Christmas Chimes

With sleigh bells in vogue for decorative purposes, here's an idea to utilize them for a group or team. The chapter on "Decorations" tells where bells might be obtained, or, you may use the toy variety sold in any department store. Suspend a wooden hoop from the ceiling or from an open doorway, and hang the sleigh bells in the middle of this hoop. Arrange two teams at a distant point and have the players take turns trying to throw a ball at the bells in the hoop. Each time the "chimes" are struck, the player is credited with 10 points. If the ball goes through the hoop but does not cause a tinkling of the bells, the pitcher receives 5 points. The game is continued until one of the teams scores a total of 200 points.

A Bubble Blowing Contest
Because soap bubbles with their many colors are suggestive of Christmas balls, this old favorite will fit in nicely as a team game. Divide the group into the Blues and the Reds with a leader for each side. At one end of a long table place the goals, which may be pencils stuck into cotton spools. Cover the table with a couple of old shawls or flannel. Do not fasten the cloth as it may become necessary to remove it in order to let it dry. After the game has progressed a few minutes it may be necessary to remove the top cover since the bubbles are apt to stick when they come to a damp spot.

The idea is to blow the bubbles along the surface of the table and through the goal posts at the end. The leader of one team "serves" the bubbles by dropping them from the pipe on the table. The players take turns blowing the delicate spheres with the idea of having them pass through the goal. After four rounds the side with the most goals is declared the winner.

Holiday Diary
Pass paper pads and pencils among the guests, and have each person record his doings of the preceding Christmas, New Year's Day and Thanksgiving. Collect the impromptu diaries and place them in a large vase or bowl. Have the players, one by one, draw a slip and read it aloud. The results are apt to be slightly embarrassing, and at the same time will engender a lot of fun.

The Gift Game
Provide each guest with a pencil and paper. Instruct him to make a sentence of four words, using words beginning with these letters G-I-F-T, allowing five or ten minutes for the game. For example: George Invited Fay Thursday. The contestant having the best sentence, in the opinion of a previously appointed board of judges, may be awarded an inexpensive gift.

Christmas Art

Distribute pencils and paper to the guests. Turn out the lights and ask each person to draw a Santa Claus. While the room is still dark, instruct them to draw reindeer and a sleigh for jolly old St. Nick. The lights are then turned on and the papers collected for exhibit. Appoint a judge to award a prize for the best artistic effort in the collection.

Christmas Candle Relay

Divide the guests into two teams placed on opposite sides of the room, and give each team a lighted candle. One at a time the players must carry the lighted candle to the opposite side of the room and back again, handing it to the person next in line. Each player must complete the trip with the candle lighted, no matter how many times he has to relight it. The team that finishes first is the winner. Each member might be awarded a small chocolate Santa Claus.

CHRISTMAS QUIZZES

Questions and answers will be popular so long as human beings like to preen their I.Q.s before an audience. Here are four Quiz programs on an educational basis, and another which, frankly, may be classified as riddles or conundrums clothed in holiday garb.

True or False Quiz

In this group you ask your guests to designate, on paper, the status of the following, either *True* or *False:*

1. Our Puritan forefathers clung to all the Christmas traditions of Merrie Old England. (False.)
2. There are towns in the United States named Santa Claus and Christmas. (True. Santa Claus is in Indiana, and Christmas is in Florida.)
3. There is only one island called Christmas Island. (False. There are three islands named "Christmas.")
4. The festival of St. Nicholas first took place on December 25th. (False. December 6th is correct.)
5. First definite traces of Christmas celebrations were found in the second century, A.D. (True.)

THE CHRISTMAS PARTY   53

6. The old belief was that bread made on Christmas Day became mouldy. (False. It was believed never to become mouldy.)

7. If a flat-footed woman or barefooted person entered a house when the Yule Log was burning, it was considered good luck. (False.)

8. The custom of serving hot punch at midnight to guests in English hotels has been discontinued in the twentieth century. (False.)

Do You Know?

Ask your group if they know these interesting facts about the holiday season:

1. What famous scientist whose first name is Isaac, was born on Christmas in the year 1642? (Sir Isaac Newton.)
2. What colorful fête of a summer flower is held on January first, and where? (Fête of Roses in Pasadena, California.)
3. In what favorite sport do the English indulge on Boxing Day? (Fox Hunting.)
4. By whom was the celebration of Christmas considered a punishable offense until the Church of England established Christmas services in Boston? (Early Puritans in late 17th century.)
5. On what day was it once considered lucky ror Christmas to fall? (Sunday.)
6. If the sun shone brightly in rural England at noon on Christmas Day, what fruit was destined to have a plentiful crop? (Apples.)
7. What were mutton pies? (Mince pies were called mutton pies in old England.)
8. Does the Bible narrative of the Nativity state that three kings came to rejoice at the birth of Christ? (They were not kings but Magi and the number was not restricted to three.)

Take Your Choice

The players are to put on paper the correct answers.

1. Waits are (a) used for measuring—(b) people who are kept waiting—(c) *Christmas carolers.*
2. Boxing Day in England is (a) the day the championship boxing match takes place—(b) *the day after Christmas*—(c) Christmas Eve.

3. The early Christians celebrated Christmas in (a) *January*— (b) *May*—(c) *April*—(d) December. (Three different months at various periods in history.)

4. The custom of trimming the Christmas tree was taken from (a) the Romans—(b) *the Germans*—(c) the Scandinavians.

5. St. Nicholas was the patron saint of (a) Italy—(b) *Russia*—(c) Germany.

Fill in the Missing Letters

These sentences are based on information found elsewhere in this book.

1. The -h-i--m-s c---l has its -r-g-n b--o-e the f---t--n-- c-nt--y.
2. Gift giving in -r-nc- is a feature of N-w --a-'s --y.
3. Instead of -ant- C--u-, the ch-l---- in -taly have a-in-ly o-d --dy c-ll-- Bef--a.
4. In the ---g--ge of -ra---, Santa Cl-us is c---ed "P--- N--l."
5. -um-er- still g-v- a traditional play about S-. G-or-e and the -ra-o- in many places in England.
6. The custom of bearing in the -o-r's -e-d at Christmas is still observed at Queen's College, Oxford.

Complete sentences will be found on page 55.

In a Much Lighter Vein!

Q. What falls but never gets hurt?
A. *Snow.*
Q. Can you spell hard water with three letters?
A. *I-c-e.*
Q. Why is snow different from Sunday?
A. *Snow can fall any day in the week.*
Q. Why is the ocean like plum pudding?
A. *They both contain currants. (Currents)*
Q. Why is a stick of Christmas candy like a horse?
A. *The more you lick it the faster it goes.*
Q. Which is the faster, heat or cold?
A. *Heat must be, because you can catch cold.*
Q. When is a ship like a huge pile of snow?
A. *When it is adrift.*
Q. What is that which is seen three times in each week, **twice** in every day but only once in a year?

A. *The letter E.*
Q. What can everybody do at the same time?
A. *Grow older.*
Q. How can you keep a rooster from crowing on Christmas?
A. *Chop off his head the day before.*

* * * * * * *

Here are the sentences in the MISSING LETTER quiz. For the eyes of the judge only!

1. The Christmas carol has its origin before the fourteenth century.
2. Gift giving in France is a feature of New Year's Day.
3. Instead of Santa Claus, the children in Italy have a kindly old lady called Befana.
4. In the language of Brazil, Santa Claus is called "Papa Noël."
5. Mummers still give a traditional play about St. George and the Dragon in many places in England.
6. The custom of bearing in the boar's head at Christmas is still observed at Queen's College, Oxford.

GAMES AND PARTIES FOR CHILDREN

Christmas belongs to the children. This is the best time of the year for arranging a party for boys and girls of all ages. Even the toddler is old enough to enjoy taking part. Indeed, when the *Four-to-Six-Year-Old Youngsters* assemble for fun and frolic, the leader can be pretty certain that the affair is going to be a happy momentous occasion. Contrary to popular belief, children of tender years are not difficult to entertain if the leaders bear in mind that the members of the group have just grown out of babyhood, and arrange the program accordingly.

The games should be simple, repetitive and not too exciting. In selecting stunts, avoid any that might cause a fall or require much running about. "Blindfold" games, or those requiring sticks or pointed objects that might lead to injury, should not be used. Remember, too, that the younger children are apt to be timid until they are told exactly what to do. Another thing, see that the games call for the participation of everyone and that each participant receives a prize, if rewards are given. Also, as soon as the children have removed their wraps, see that there is a chair for each one and that conditions which induce pushing, crowding or squirming are eliminated as nearly as possible.

Action games are popular among children in the *Seven-to-Eleven-Year Group*. They have their first "grown-up" feeling and the school bell has beckoned them to a new world, filled with activities heretofore unknown. For the first time, many of them are meeting and mingling socially with others of the same age. They become friendly and the inherent traits of activity are manifested. This leads to the awakening of a new spirit, which may be satisfied in a program which is lively and highly competitive.

The *Twelve-to-Fifteen-Year Group* is a difficult one for which to arrange a Christmas celebration. These advanced grade-school students and high school freshmen are young men and women, if you please. They resent being treated as children and do not readily take to programs that are juvenile in their scope. For this reason many of the games described in the party section for adults may be used also.

An Old-Fashioned Children's Party

The decorative scheme might be red and green, with equal numbers of red and green inflated balloons suspended from the ceiling, or from the sides of the room if the ceiling is too high for easy accessibility. In the windows set red candles in green wreaths, and trim the windows and sills with intertwined red and green crepe paper, and drape the lighting fixtures with the same materials. In one end of the room place the Christmas tree. Trim it with candy canes, strings of pink and white popcorn and assorted Christmas balls. The table for refreshments may be covered with a holiday paper spread, on sale at the five-and-ten or at almost any department store. In the center of the table place three bowls in a triangle, and fill them with oranges, apples and grapes. Bank the bowls with sprigs of holly, bits of evergreen and pine cones. Tie "Christmas imprinted napkins" with thin ribbons of green paper, and at each place lay a bundle of mints wrapped in green cellophane.

As soon as the guests arrive, start the suggested program of games and stunts, all of which are described elsewhere in this chapter. Begin with "Find the Christmas Tree," a junior ice breaker, if the age is under twelve. Substitute the warming-up game entitled "Heil Holiday" (p. 44) if the children are older.

Proceed with the following games:

> Hanging the Christmas Stocking (p. 58)
> Ring the Bell (p. 59)
> Musical Wreath (p. 60)
> Christmas Ball Relay (p. 61)
> Balloon Blowing Contest (p. 62)

After these five games, announce the fact that Santa Claus will soon be here. With this welcome news, distribute small pieces of paper or cards bearing different numbers. After Santa arrives and is comfortably fixed, the children go up to him, one by one, and present their numbered cards. The jovial old fellow reaches into his bag and gives the child a package bearing the same number as the one he has just surrendered. The gifts need not be expensive. Ten-cent articles are appreciated, and besides, half the fun comes in opening the well-wrapped packages.

Following the distribution of gifts, the children sing, to the tune of "Happy Birthday to You!" the following:

> Merry Christmas to You!
> Merry Christmas to You!
> Merry Christmas, Dear Santa,
> Merry Christmas to You!

If there are a few minutes remaining, here is a good spot to conduct "The Junior Christmas Quiz."

For older children the following games are also suggested:

> Christmas Plum Pudding
> Christmas in the Barnyard
> Candle Quoits
> Your Favorite Animal

In pairing the guests for the march to the refreshment table, use the game titled "Christmas Animals." As soon as the boys and girls have found their partners, they gather around the festive board and enjoy ice cream, cake, fruit and holiday candies and nuts.

Games for Four-to-Six-Year Groups

Find the Christmas Tree

Hide several small Christmas trees, of the five-and-ten variety, in various places in the room. It will be a diplomatic maneuver to have one tree for each child present. Instruct the children to find a tree and then return to a chair and await the arrival of the others with their trees. When each has found a tree, everyone is to sing out, "Merry Christmas to all!"

Hanging the Christmas Stocking

This is a variation of the game known as "Pinning the Donkey's Tail." While we cautioned against blindfold games in general, this might be considered an exception since there is no danger of injury if the children are watched by the leaders in charge. Blindfold each in turn and place a real or paper stocking in the hand, with a pin at the top. Turn the player around and send him in the direction of a real or improvised mantel. Stretch a cloth over the mantel so that the stocking may be easily hung. The one who hangs the stocking in the best position will be declared the winner of a small stocking of toys, with each of the other children receiving an individual piece of candy.

A Junior Christmas Quiz

The mother or party leader will ask the following question in typical "Uncle Jim" style. If the children are of early school age, the Quiz could be in the form of a competition; if they are younger than five or six, the idea of sides or team points should be eliminated. Here are the questions:

1. Where do you find icicles at Christmas? (On buildings or shrubbery outside, or on the tree inside.)
2. Where do you find cranberries at Christmas? (Strung on the tree or on the dinner table.)
3. Where do you find bright ribbon at Christmas time? (On the gift package.)
4. Where do you find snow at Christmas? (On the tree, or perhaps, on the ground outside.)

5. What do you usually find in the toe of a Christmas stocking. (An orange.)

6. What color balls are there on the tree? (Red, green and other colors depending on the tree at the party.)

7. Do you ever see Christmas trees growing near your home? (Probably, "Yes.")

8. What are the colors of the lights on the tree? (Usually red, green, orange and blue.)

9. Where do you hang your stocking Christmas Eve? (Over the fireplace or mantel.)

10. Do you know what many naughty children find in their stocking Christmas morning? (A piece of coal.)

11. What colors do you see most at Christmas? (Red and green.)

12. What do these colors mean if you are riding in a car or crossing a street? (Red means "Stop" and green means "Go.")

Ring the Bell

Suspend a bell from the ceiling on a red ribbon or cord. Have the children blindfolded before they take turns groping for the bell. When the bell is located the youngster rings it long and loud until the blindfold is removed, and he is presented with a candy toy bell.

Stringing Popcorn

Give each child a handful of colored candy popcorn. Distribute store string and a large needle and have them string the grains. The child who finishes first will receive a box of cracker jack candy or some similar reward.

Color Grab Bag Game

The materials required include white paper, paste, crayons, a large sheet of wrapping paper and seasonal illustrations from December magazines and newspapers. Cut out such figures as Christmas trees, Santa Claus, Christmas wreaths, candy canes, reindeer, Yule bells and candles. Use these cutouts to trace around on white paper. Then, have the children cut out these white traced figures and paste on a large piece of wrapping paper. Pin this wrapping paper to the wall. Now, take the small figures and put them in a hat. Pass it around among the children and have each draw one. The figure chosen is the one the child is to color on the large picture. (wrapping paper.)

Musical Wreath

The only material needed is a large wreath. A real one may be purchased or one may be improvised for the occasion. Have the tallest boy and girl hold this wreath high above the heads of the children as they pass under it, to the music of "Jingle Bells." When the radio or piano stops, the boy and girl drop the wreath over the child who happens to be directly under it. The captured child is eliminated from the procession. This continues until the last child is caught. He should receive a small prize for his good fortune or expertness in escaping.

What's in the Package?

To start the game have one of the older children leave the room. Then choose another of the group to be a Christmas package. Have the child sit on a chair and cover him with white tissue paper loosely tied together with red ribbon. The packaging will be sure to tickle those who are helping with the bundle. All of the remaining children now hide in a room located in a different direction from the one where the older child is waiting to be called.

Call him in and have him guess who is in the package. This can continue until several children have had a chance to guess the identity of the one chosen to represent the package.

Santa's Treat

Distribute small pieces of paper or cards bearing different numbers. At one end of the room have your assistant dressed as Santa Claus behind a table where packages of various shapes and sizes have been placed. Instruct the children to go up to Santa Claus one by one and present their number. The jovial old fellow with the patriarchal beard will then give the child a package bearing the same number as the one surrendered by the child. The gifts need not be expensive. Any ten-cent article will be appreciated with half the fun coming in opening the well-wrapped package.

Games for Seven-to-Eleven-Year Groups

Bottle the Popcorn

The materials required are a quart milk bottle and a quantity of popcorn. Place the milk jar on the floor in the center of the room. Give each player, who stands at the end of the room, ten grains of popcorn and have each participant attempt to drop them, one by one, into the neck of the bottle. The idea is, of course, to see how many each can drop into the container. See to it that each child stands erect when he takes his aim.

A Santa Puzzle

Draw a Santa Claus on a large piece of paper. Cut the picture into pieces so that there will be three or four parts for each child present. Distribute the sections and have the boys and girls circle around a card table where they will try to re-assemble Old Santa in typical jig-saw puzzle style.

Christmas Ball Relay

Line your participants in two even teams. Place a large Christmas ball in the hand of each captain, who stands at the head of the line. When the signal is given, the children holding the Christmas globes run to the end of the line and hand them to the last player. He runs to the front of the line to give it to the next player, and so on until the ball finally gets back to the captain. The captain retrieving the ball first wins the game for his side.

Snow-Ball Throw

This is a popular group game for seven-to-eleven-year-old youngsters.

Designate one of the party to walk up and down the room and try to intercept a large snow-ball, made of cotton, as it is tossed about by the girls and boys. When the child who is IT is fortunate enough to intercept the cotton ball, he takes the chair of the one who threw the intercepted pass. The game continues with the one who threw the ball now attempting to make the interception and thereby regain his seat. This game may go on for a limited time. It is usually a lot of fun for five or six minutes.

Balloon Blowing Contest

Divide the children into two teams and place the teams at opposite ends of the room. The children at one end will be known as the "Green" club and each will be presented with a large sized (deflated) green balloon. The players at the other end of the room will be supplied with a large (deflated) red balloon and this group will be known as the "Red" club.

At a given signal the balloons are to be blown up and tied with a piece of string. Then, the object of the game is to keep the balloons moving in the air toward the opposite goal. The first team whose players succeed in advancing all of the balloons to the opposite part of the room, will be declared the winning combination. The balloons are propelled to the goal line by patting or pushing them with one hand while the other hand is held behind the back.

Santa's Helpers

This is a nice way to present your young guests with a favor. Give a stocking to each child, filled with an orange, apple, dates, candy, nuts and small toys. At a given signal all are to empty their stockings as quickly as possible and hang them on the mantel or over the fireplace. A piece of heavy muslin may be stretched across the mantel for the convenience of the children in pinning the stockings. Tell them to fill the stockings again, with the winner accorded the honor of leading the march to the dining room.

Unpacking the Present

Place an inexpensive gift in a small bag or box. Wrap paper around the parcel until you have a dozen or more wrappings, each securely and separately fastened. With the players in a circle, the parcel is started around as someone tunes in music on the radio or begins to play the piano. While the music is being played, the parcel is moved from hand to hand, but as soon as it stops, the player holding the parcel starts to unwrap it. The break in the music should be frequent but only for a few seconds at a time. When the music starts again, the parcel is passed along. This is continued until the package is finally unwrapped. The player who uncovers the present is allowed to keep it as his prize.

Games for Twelve-to-Fifteen-Year Groups

Christmas Plum Pudding

All players are seated in a circle with the exception of the one who is IT. He stands in the middle of the group and fires this question at one of the players: "What shall I eat with my Christmas pudding?" The one who has been asked the question must answer with something good to eat beginning with the letter C *before* the one who asks the question is finished counting up to ten. If no answer is forthcoming within the stipulated period, the hesitating player exchanges places with the interrogator.

The Christmas "Chew Chew"

Have your young guests write their names on slips of paper. Place the names of the girls in one receptacle and the names of the boys in another. Pass the container with the boys' slips to the girls and each draws out a name. (*Or* pass the girls' names to the young gentlemen in the game.) Now, tell them to find the partners they drew.

Next, explain that before the party started you hid a candy cane with a long piece of string for every couple present. Tell the partners to find the cane and string, tie the cane in the middle of the string, put an end of the string in the mouth and start chewing until the cane is reached. The couple who finishes first may be awarded small souvenir canes for their chewing skill.

Christmas in the Barnyard

Write the names of the common animals and fowls on small slips of paper, and distribute them among the guests. Some suggestions for animals: cow, horse, pig, dog, cat, donkey, sheep, duck, rooster, hen, turkey gobbler.

Conceal the lower part of the faces with a large handkerchief. One of the group stands in the middle of the room and cries: "Merry Christmas to all in the barnyard!" With the faces well concealed behind the handkerchiefs, each member of the barnyard flock answers with the sound which characterizes the animal or fowl he represents. If the one in the center can distinguish a sound made and the person who made it, he then exchanges places with that person.

Candle Quoits

Place a long red candle in a crepe-covered flower pot, filled with dirt. Make five rings of wired tinsel and have the crowd take turns throwing them over the candle. Each ringer will count two points. The player with the highest score after three rounds of tossing, will be the winner.

Christmas Roulette

Take the four-numeral spinner from a ten-cent game and paste pieces of paper over the numbers. Print on one "X*mas Tree*"; another, "X*mas Gifts*"; another, "X*mas Dinner*" and on the fourth, "X*mas Decorations.*"

Seat your players in a circle around the wheel. Spin it with vigor and gusto. When the wheel stops, the "croupier" calls out the subject and the name of a player he wishes to name something with the subject. For instance, the point of the spinner stops on *Xmas Tree*. The leader calls out "Christmas tree, Mary Johnson!" Mary must reply with one of the following words: tinsel, lights, bulbs, toys, icicles, or something similar. If the spinner points to *Xmas Dinner*, the leader shouts, "Christmas Dinner, Jimmie Crompton!" He replies with one of the following: cranberries, turkey, gravy, plum pudding, mince pie, celery, etc. The answer must be given before the leader counts *ten*.

Your Favorite Animal

Place a mirror, well-covered with a cloth, in a small room, all the while making an extravagant display of secrecy, so that the whole business appears most mysterious. Announce that you are going to reproduce a picture of the player's favorite animal. Lead each guest, one by one, into the room and stand him before the covered looking glass. Ask him what animal he would like to see. After he has decided he wants to see a monkey, a mule, a hyena or what not, you raise the cloth and he will see HIMSELF.

Making a Santa Claus

Each player at the party will get a thrill out of making a Santa Claus. The methods and materials are simple and inexpensive. Cut away the outside shell of a cornstalk until the pith is reached. Then give to each a piece of the pith, about six inches long. Give instructions to whittle out one end to resemble a head. Tell them to draw Santa's face on the head with pen and ink. Next, glue one half of a lead ball (used for fishing weights and obtainable at the hardware store) on the lower end of the pith. Have them make Santa's costume out of crepe paper, red for his suit and blue for his hat. With the weight in the bottom of the figure, jolly Old St. Nick will always stand upright.

Christmas Push

Place a large Christmas ball and a teacup side by side on the table. Tell your guests to take turns in attempting to push the ball through the handle of the cup. When they fail to understand how it is done, you simply put your finger through the handle and push the ball.

Mrs. Santa Claus' Reception

Here is a party plan which grew—as all good party plans must grow, out of imagination. It takes a basic idea, that of the farewell party by Mrs. Santa Claus to the toys and dolls made by Santa Claus and ready to go out to the boys and girls for Christmas. It uses the form of some familiar games, adapting them to this idea, and invents new games. It can be used for children, will be even more appreciated by the young people and will be hilarious for adults. While designed for Christmas, it has been gloriously successful at a Summer Camp in August.

INVITATIONS

On long sheets of paper—cream-colored is suggested—write or type the following Jingle. Decorate the sheet with Santa Claus stickers and use a sticker to fasten it when folded.

> Out of the shop of Santa Claus
>   Go all the dolls and toys,
> Welcomed all over the world, because
>   They are bringers of Christmas joys.
>
> But don't you think that the Christmas toys
>   Themselves should have some fun
> Ere their task of pleasing the girls and boys
>   Is at Christmas-time begun?

Mrs. Santa Claus thinks so too
So she sends this message inviting you
To the Santa Claus Shop, where in formal state
The Toys Reception begins at eight.
Bring a ten-cent toy with you—
                                And don't be late!

Place ....
Date ....

The social room should be a gay reproduction of what you might imagine the shope of Santa Claus to look like. Over the entrance have a sign—

CHRISTMAS TOY SHOP

LATEST MODELS—DOLLS AND TOYS

S. Claus—*Proprietor*

Decorate the walls with huge poster pictures of toys, in bright colors, red predominating. The pictures may be sketched roughly or made by cutting a toy out of colored paper and pasting it on a contrastingly colored poster. Small toys can be fastened on posters, so can ginger cookie men, animal crackers, etc. Have an empty table or two to hold the toys brought by the guests, which will be temporarily part of the decoration and then sent to an orphanage, hospital or other place where toys are needed. Small Christmas trees can be hung with candy toys and candy canes. An exhibit of dolls, loaned by the young women in the group, would be interesting. (Collecting dolls from different countries is, by the way, a fascinating hobby. I know! It's my hobby.) Paper dolls can be used effectively for decoration.

Refreshments can be served from a Noah's Ark built of compo-board or even constructed of sheets hung over wire with colored roof and windows of paper pinned on. Mrs. Santa Claus should be a chubby person (her costume will make her so, if Nature hasn't) in bright red muslin dress with a white apron, white hair and cap and spectacles. Her assistants, the members of the social committee, should be dressed as workmen in overalls or smocks. Mr. Santa Claus will wear the usual costume but will not appear at the beginning of the program.

Refreshments should be colored fruit punch (use grape juice for color or the pure vegetable coloring sold by reliable grocers), gingerbread men, animal crackers, candy toys and canes, or lollipops and stick candy if the party is out of season.

PROGRAM

1. March of the Toys
2. Engine Relay
3. The Doll Shop
4. Top Twirl
5. Drawing Contest
6. Story Book Show
7. Parade of the Wooden Soldiers
8. Jumping Jacks

March of the Toys

After Mrs. Santa Claus has welcomed the guests they will be allowed about ten minutes to turn themselves into toys. For this purpose they may draw two articles from a table of supplies on which will be provided strips of colored crepe paper (for hair-ribbons for dolls or neckties for clowns), string (you might be a top and wind yourself up), old keys (so that you can be a mechanical toy), whistles (if you prefer to be a steam engine), old roller-skate wheels, etc. Each player may use two articles to indicate what he represents but no more than two. When the toys are ready a lively march will be played and all the toys will march past Mr. Santa Claus who has by this time made a stately entrance driving his reindeer. He will award a toy prize to the best representation and put the least clever through some stunts. He may, for instance, suggest that they need more glue and have them try to feed each other (blindfolded) soft molasses taffies.

If preferred, the guests may come to the party dressed as dolls or wooden soldiers. This plan makes a much jollier and more colorful party and the young people of the two camps where I tried it out loved the idea. They turned themselves into the most amazing dolls with only the contents of a camper's suitcase to help them.

Engine Relay

The difficulty with mechanical toys is that they are apt to be balky when wound up. The engine race is a relay, with the entire group divided into four teams. They line up at one end of the room and the first player in each line starts at the signal toward a mark at the other end of the room. All the while he goes he must make a noise suggesting some kind of engine, the "Chug-chug" of a locomotive, the "Clang! Clang!" of a fire-engine, etc. And instead of racing directly forward he must go forward six steps, then back two, two to right, then two to left, repeating the process to the goal and back to the line where he touches off the next player who will proceed in the same way. The first line to have every player back in place wins.

The Doll Shop

While the Engine Relay is going on have about ten of the guests preparing the next stunt—"The Doll Shop"—during which Santa will be salesman and one of the players the customer. Each of the others will represent a different kind of doll—a walking doll, jigging doll, talking doll, baby doll, even a broken doll could be included. Santa will show the customer each doll, and the customer will find fault with each until at last one pleases him and he goes off with it under his arm.

Top Twirl

Divide the entire company into groups of two, each player being either the Top or the String with the exception of about six or more players who are Strings whose Tops have been lost. Top and String will clasp right hands facing each other. At the first whistle of the leader String will run around Top, turning Top as he runs. At the second whistle String stands still while Top twirls around, at the third whistle Tops suddenly stop and hold up their right hands while each String rushes to get a new Top. Some Strings will, of course, be left and will wait until the next time to try to catch a Top. No String may have the same Top twice. This will be especially good fun if a rollicking tune is played on the piano and the Tops hum the tune while spinning.

Drawing Contest

Four lines of about eight each are lined up facing a blackboard (or four large posters) as far away as the size of the room permits. At the starter's signal the first person in each line runs forward and draws the head of Santa Claus, who is posing for his portrait. After

THE CHRISTMAS PARTY 69

drawing the artist hurries back to give his chalk or crayon to the next member of his team who puts in Santa Claus's features. The next player adds his neck, the next his body, the next his arms, the next his feet, the last the finishing touches. The winning team must be judged for the artistic effect of the portrait as well as the speed with which it was completed.

Story Book Show

Divide the entire party into groups of from six to ten and give each group a turn at acting out a familiar children's story in a pantomime. This may be done directly in front of the audience in darkness and a light back of the players.

Parade of the Wooden Soldiers

The entire company will line up in a single file and march stiffly and with jerky steps and absolutely solemn faces past Santa Claus, while the "Parade of the Wooden Soldiers" is played slowly. Santa by making faces or remarks will endeavor to make the soldiers laugh as they pass and repass him. Each soldier who laughs must leave the line. The last to remain in line should be awarded a black crepe band for his arm—high honor in the Legion of Wooden Heads!

Jumping Jacks

A race for four to ten players, each player proceeding from start to goal with the following movement—hands on hips, deep knee bend, jump forward. Straighten up, deep knee bend, jump forward.

NOTE: The game Mrs. Santa Claus is from "Stunts of All Lands" by Catherine Atkinson Miller, used by permission of Harper and Brothers, New York, N. Y.

DECORATIONS

SCHOOL, CHURCH AND SOCIAL HALL

THE IMPORTANCE of decorating the school, church or hall in the spirit of the occasion cannot be over-emphasized. Wherever the Christmas entertainment is held, there should be a tree, covered with colorful lights, glistening with artificial snow and laden with Christmas balls. In every group there are persons who know how to trim the tree artistically for the enjoyment of all who attend.

One way to decorate the school is to transform the classroom or auditorium into a forest scene. Give the pupils an opportunity to display their own creative and artistic talents and you will be surprised at the unusual results. Garlands of greens and berries, if possible, can be draped from the lighting fixture to the corners of the room. Have the class artist decorate the blackboards with outdoor scenes. If a large tree is to be in one corner of the room, the scenes on the blackboards should be arranged in a sequence so that the last drawing would appear to lead to the tree. For example: The first board would be a woodland road, snow laden trees, snowy banks and Santa, sled and reindeer; next, the village scene with steeple of a church rising above the other dwellings, a cottage or small house with wreaths in the windows; third, a wild-life scene, with animals scurrying to cover; and last, the board leading to the tree would be either the Christmas wreath or three bells wishing all, "Merry Christmas."

The tree itself could be transformed into a snowy one by spraying it with soapsuds and then sprinkling it with artificial snow. Where the teacher or leader is giving presents, these remembrances should be tied on the tree in red and green cellophane or whatever color scheme is predominant. Window sills covered with pine boughs make a perfect nest for rich pine cones tied with bright red ribbon. To carry out the woodland atmosphere, rabbits, squirrels and other small animals could be peeping from the pine forest. Effective finishing touches consist of garlands of green festooned around or outlining entire windows tied with red cellophane bows. The plain green wreath is also very impressive.

The Crib Scene

Where the Child in the Manger is substituted for the Christmas tree, the blackboards may carry Biblical scenes, with the shepherds tending their sheep, the wise men on their camels, and finally the Star of Bethlehem with its ray falling on the crib. A stall can be made of poles, with the floor banked with mountains of green paper and overhead, branches of any Christmas greens available. The straw for the little manger can be placed on an ordinary trunk rack. If the room is small and time and expense is a factor, the teacher's desk may be used for building the crib scene on a miniature scale.

Serve refreshments on a table with white cloth, garlanded with greens and the ever-appropriate holly with its colorful berries. The center decorations may be a circle of holly, a Christmas wreath or left-overs of the greens used in trimming the room—and fill the circle with Christmas balls or assorted fruit.

HOME TABLE DECORATIONS

Set the table in buffet style, using silver-tones cellophane to simulate ice. In the center, or at both ends if the table is long, place oval mirrors, covering the frame with fringe of cotton sprinkled with the frosted snow, obtainable at any novelty store. Then have a reindeer and sleigh or skating figures gliding over the mirror. Clip these winter scenes out of colored advertisements in the national magazines, and paste them on cardboard so that they will stand erect. Place two or more evergreen trees around the skating scene. A toy Santa Claus makes an appropriate favor.

OUTDOORS

Make your outdoor trimmings so soul-satisfying and charming that they will cheer the passer-by as his eyes feast on the twinkling candles in the windows and the beauty of the decorated doors, trees and house. Sharing your decorations with others at Christmastide increases your joy twofold: you get pleasure out of it, and it does good to the hearts and souls of those who drive or walk by your home.

Guard against over-decoration, for it spoils everything: it is better to highlight the graceful prettiness of a blue spruce on the lawn or the exquisite architectural details of a door. Last year a thoughtful owner of an estate decorated his gateposts with a sheaf of pine and strings of cones tied with huge red bows of oiled silk. At nightfall the entrance lights cast cheery shadows on the posts, and the glitter of falling snow against the charming background was a sight no one would want to miss. It takes but a few minutes to bind carefully the pine branches with fine wire. Cones should be strung as one would arrange gourds, so that the rich brown nestles in a bed of green above which you tie the bow. If oiled silk is not available, you may well substitute red oilcloth or any other material suitable for outdoors.

Where is the man or woman who does not sigh with envy at the sight of a glamorous holly tree? I am speaking of the perfect specimen which you sometimes see on the spacious lawn of a suburban estate—the "twelve-footer." With a six- or eight-foot spread, bedecked with clusters of red berries and girdled with colored electric bulbs, a huge star at the top flashing the glad message, Merry Christmas to All!

Another method of illuminating the holly tree calls for blue lights and frosty white tip-shaped candles. Some owners, however, favor red and white lights or glowing white and blue globular bulbs.

It is suggested that entrance pillars be encircled with greens and that the arch be likewise garlanded. One bright star at the peak will electrify the entire scene and emphasize the beauty of the wreath with its red bow outside the door. Potted evergreens draped with circular strings of electric lights leading to another light in the shape of a star complete this gay picture.

If your house is small, here is a suggestion: Design and make an over-the-door spray, in the center of which cluster bright red and frosty white Christmas-tree balls.

For the door whose architectural beauty needs very little enhancing a Christmas wreath may be placed above it and in the center, from which plain green garlands may fall—the two outer strips touching the floor and the two on either side of the door dropping three-quarter length. With the light shining through the glass there will be sufficient illumination to welcome arriving guests and give joy to the passer-by.

If your Colonial house boasts a graceful balcony, spread the Christmas decorations by Yuletide tie-back draperies and festoon the entire window framing with greens and shiny bright red balls. A brightly lighted potted tree may be placed in the center.

For floral decorations that are beautiful, lasting, non-inflammable and not affected by water, etc., there is a new material known as Florafilm which has been developed by the Tensolite Laboratory, 33 Kelbourne Avenue, in Tarrytown, N. Y. This material is easily handled and comes in a variety of colors (and combinations of colors) in various weights and width, with or without beaded edges, and in special forms for petals, leaves, stems, centers, etc. While intended primarily for table, hair, corsage and package ornaments, it can also be used for many purposes such as favors, hat trimming, doll dressing, basketry, weaving, crocheting, costuming and packages.

A ribbon similar to this material (also developed by the Tensolite Laboratory) is noted for its beauty and excellent tying quality. This new ribbon is available in most stores under the name, Plioribbon.

A liberal sample of Florafilm will be forwarded to those interested in its application who write to the above-mentioned concern.

Another outstanding decoration is a special strap of sleigh bells to be used in connection with Christmas door wreaths. The bells on this strap are made from pure cast bell metal (copper and tin) in assorted sizes and mounted on full grain leather straps. These straps may be hung either on or beside the door, or they may be arranged in any shape to conform with the door casings or the leaded windows. The manufacturer of these door bells is Bevin Brothers Manufacturing Company, East Hampton, Connecticut.

INDOORS

You may add holiday cheer to the indoors by beginning in the center hall entrance. Drape the casings of the stairs with green garlands caught up here and there with bunches of red holly berries fastened by red bows or lustrous tree balls. The newel post lends itself naturally to clever schemes. One way is to garland round and round and then top it with a poinsettia, or a small, potted Christmas evergreen with or without lights. A bowl of brightly hued gourds from which flow fiesta fruits, gourds, peppers, etc., suggests the anticipated feast. A pine bough tied with red ribbon fastening the rich brown cones into an attractive spray will completely screen the entire newel post.

The doorways leading from this entrance should be given attention. This can be done by hanging the wreath directly in the center and then green-garlanding down either side, completely outlining each doorway. Where there is a center fixture this may be decorated effectively with clusters of small holly sprigs.

Mirrors are helpful, both for beauty and reflection. Treat the one over the table in the hall with a handmade frame of holly or pungent boxes of sumac and bayberries tied with a soft, lustrous red satin bow—preferably in the lower right corner. This gives the mirror more space for reflection.

The table with a highly polished surface may be arranged with crystal drop candlesticks holding stately white tapers at each end. The centerpiece is a small skeleton tree set on a mirror. The branches are fashioned from heavy strands of wire covered with twisted white florists' tape from which hang small gleaming blue and white frosted tree balls—with the tree itself completely reflected in the mirror.

Let us turn to the living room with its fireplace and broad window sills. This is indeed a background for a decorative spree! One home, which delighted the children, possessed a small tree with cotton toy animals in each window, so wired that a single star illuminated the window after dark. One window represented the Christmas Manger with the Christ-child, the Holy Family with all the animals and a few of the celestial chorus watching the nearby shepherds. The second was a village scene with tiny inhabitants going through the deep snow to the church, with its stained glass windows, spires and bell tower. Everything was complete, even to the straggling dog following its little mistress. The third was a forest scene with glistening snow covering the trees and little birds pecking away at their Christmas dinner. A miniature pool in the background was made from a pocket mirror, with the inevitable stag at the "water's edge."

When bayberry candles are used, tuck them safely in a bed of evergreens and thereby carry out the old legend on Christmas Eve:

"A Bayberry candle burned to its socket
Brings food to the larder,
Health to the home,
And wealth to the pocket."

Wrap the Christmas plants in bright red cellophane fastened with sprigs of green holly or green ribbon, or some other color scheme in harmony with your own plans and ideas.

The arrangement of the Christmas tree is decidedly an individual project, with each having his own ideas regarding the most artistic method of trimming. In more homes each year the live tree is making its appearance. After the holidays are over, the younger members of the family will delight in removing it from the pot and transplanting it to the lawn.

When you arrange decorations for the dinner table, always

remember to keep them low enough so that conversation may be carried on easily.

For that "rush meal" on Christmas Eve it is suggested that you use a golden-yellow cloth and green-blue fiesta ware, with gleaming silver candlesticks, ornamented with small brown pine cones. On the Christmas morning table there should be a centerpiece. This can be made by grouping bright green and silver Christmas balls in a nest of white cotton, sprinkled with artificial snow. In each napkin tuck a bit of berried holly and on each plate deposit a small box containing a useful gift, wrapped in red cellophane and tied with green cellophane ribbon.

REFRESHMENTS

BECAUSE of the important place feasting occupies in the holiday festivities of all countries, we have included a collection of our favorite recipes and menus. In America, the Christmas dinner gives more pleasure than any other special occasion. It truly represents the zenith of national culinary achievement. Yet, from those authoritative gourmets who have dined abroad on December twenty-fifth, we learn that the Christmas dinners in other lands lose nothing by comparison with our own.

In preceding chapters we have already described the customs of serving food in other lands. In modern England, it might be added, the turkey, America's noble bird, has succeeded the famed fat goose in popularity, and the typical English menu now features roast turkey with all the trimmings. The first course consists of oyster soup, then the roast turkey, flanked by scalloped potatoes, braised celery, plum pudding, mince pie, fruit and a choice of beverages.

After filling the turkey, it is roasted on a spit, with the cook basting it often with butter and garnishing it with lemon and pickles as it is placed on the large platter. Here is how those famous English "stuffins" are made.

English Turkey Stuffing

Cut the flesh of a chicken into small pieces, add a pound of veal and beat into a mortar with a half pound of beef suet. Add as much crumbs of bread as needed, some mushrooms and truffles, cut small, plus a few sweet herbs and parsley, nutmeg, pepper and salt, ground mace, lemon peel, cut fine. Mix all together with the yolk of two eggs.

In France, the *réveillon*, or Christmas Eve supper at midnight is more important to the native than the Christmas dinner itself. A favorite *Menu de Réveillon* offered in many Parisian restaurants last year consisted of the following:

Consommé
Huitres
Pieds de Porc Truffes Grillés
Boudin Blanc Grillé
Perdreaux Rôtis aux Choux
Salade d'Endive
Fois Gras en Rocher
Glacé Fraise—Praline
Fromages
Petits-Fours   Fruits Glacés
Bananes   Oranges   Pommes
Café

One of the most delicious of all cakes is the small French flat cake. You can make some by following these directions:

French Christmas Cookies

½ cup butter or other shortening
¾ cup sugar
½ cup honey
2 egg yolks

¼ cup milk
1 teaspoon vanilla
3 cups sifted cake flour

Cream butter until soft, add sugar and beat each addition until light. Add honey and egg yolks and beat well. Add milk and vanilla. Add flour, a small amount at a time, beating until well blended after each addition. Chill dough until soft enough to handle easily. Roll thin on lightly floured board. Cut with sabot-shaped cooky pattern. Bake in ungreased baking sheets ten minutes in moderate oven (375° F.). Cool and frost with white or chocolate icing. This will yield three dozen small cookies.

French Chocolate Rabbits

¼ cup butter
¾ cup sugar
1 egg yolk
1 square unsweetened chocolate, melted

2 tablespoons heavy cream
1 tablespoon vanilla
1¾ cup sifted pastry flour

Cream butter until soft, add sugar gradually and beat after each addition until light and fluffy. Add egg yolk, chocolate, cream and vanilla. Mix well. Work in flour until smooth dough is formed. Chill for one hour. Roll thin on floured board. Cut with small cutter, sprinkle with sugar and bake in moderate oven (375° F.) about eleven minutes. Cool and frost if desired. The yield will be about 36 cookies.

German Christmas Cakes

Although each province of Germany has its favorite recipe for making *kuchen* or Christmas cakes, there are a few recipes with fame beyond the borders of the state in which they are most famous. For instance, there are the *Marzipan* cakes.

1 lb. sweet almonds	1 lb. powdered sugar
½ oz. bitter almonds	Rose water to flavor

Blanch almonds and spread out to dry 12 hours, then pound them as fine as flour. Mix sugar with powdered almonds, add bitter almonds, and enough rose water to make dough just soft enough to roll out. Divide amount of dough in two parts. On moulding board covered with powdered sugar, put half of the dough on this board and form into small flat round cakes, like macaroons, or in twisted forms, if desired. Other half of dough is put on board and rolled out half-inch thick. Then cut it into strips. Moisten edges of cakes with rose water and place strips around them, making a little cup. Edges of this cup may be cut in fancy shapes, like flower petals. Set these cups on greased paper on flat tin, and bake until light yellow.

Cakes are now ready for filling.

Filling for Marzipan

Mix one pound of powdered sugar with enough rose water to wet through, stir constantly until sugar is stiff. This will require about three-quarters of an hour. Then fill the little cakes and set in the oven to brown.

Platzen (*Small drop cakes*)

4 egg yolks	A pinch of cinnamon and cloves
2 cups powdered sugar	Flour to stiffen

Beat eggs until light and foamy. Stir in sugar and beat thoroughly. Add cinnamon and cloves and just enough flour to allow them to drop from spoon onto a greased tin. Leave room for them to spread on tin without touching.

Pfeffer-Nusse

4 eggs
1 lb. sugar
1 teaspoon baking powder
1 ground nutmeg

1 teaspoon ground cinnamon
1 teaspoon ground cloves
2 oz. candied lemon peel chopped fine
1 lb. flour

Beat eggs and sugar together and add baking powder and spices and beat thoroughly. Add flour, mix and knead on board. Shape dough into small balls and bake in slow oven on buttered tins.

Mexican Roast Turkey (*Amoli de Guajalote*)

Created by the Aztecs many hundreds of years ago, this dish is is still popular at Christmas. The fowl is parboiled and then roasted, after which it is smothered in rich blood-red pungent sauce. The dressing is thick with pepper, and after being poured over the turkey it is sprinkled with aromatic seeds. This mixture of turkey and peppers is eaten with *tortillas*.

Mexican Cakes (*Empanadas*)

2 cups flour
1 teaspoon baking powder
½ teaspoon salt

½ cup butter
⅓ cup milk

Mix and sift dry ingredients. Cut in butter and add milk. Roll out to ⅛ inch thick and cut into 4-inch circles. Fill with fruit mixture, moisten edges with cold water; fold over and press edges together. Fry in deep fat until brown and drain on brown paper.

Empanadas are filled with various mixtures. Here is one in which prepared or cooked pumpkin is used:

1 cup pumpkin
½ cup raisins
½ cup piñones or almonds
½ cup sugar

½ teaspoon cinnamon
½ teaspoon cloves
½ teaspoon allspice

Rub the pumpkin through a colander and add the other ingredients.

THE CHRISTMAS PARTY

MEXICAN CHRISTMAS DINNER

Menu

*

Caldo Colado

*

Suckling Pig
with Dressing, and Red Apple in Mouth

*

Turkey or Chicken, Roasted

*

Rice served with Hard-boiled Eggs
Stewed Tomatoes   *Tortillas*

*

Chopped Lettuce Salad with French Dressing

*

Buñuelos with Spiced Syrup

*

Coffee

Buñuelos *(Fried Puffs)*

2 eggs
1 cup milk
4 cups flour
¾ teaspoon salt
1 teaspoon baking powder

Sift the dry ingredients together. Beat the eggs well, add milk and stir in the dry ingredients, adding as much flour as it will absorb. Roll as thin as possible, and cut large and round with a hole punched in the middle. Fry in deep fat until golden brown. These can be served with Mexican chocolate.

Sweden is another country where holiday goodies are distinctly delicious. Christmas, known as *Jul,* is synonymous with feasting. The principal dishes are lutfish and ham. The lutfish is a species of codfish, which is cooked in cloth to prevent it flaking to pieces. It is usually served with a cream gravy and potatoes, seasoned with mustard. The sugar-cured ham, spiced three weeks in advance, is boiled on the day of the feast and served hot, usually with sausages.

Another dish invariably found on the Swedish table is porridge with rice and milk. It is customary to hide an almond in the porridge, with the belief that the one who finds it will have good luck the coming year. Other Swedish dishes served during the holidays are hogshead cheese, goose, and various nuts and sweetmeats.

Everyone is familiar with *vörtbröd* or malt bread but did you know that the most important Swedish cakes at Christmas are *pepparkakor* or ginger snaps? These are made in the shape of animals, especially goats and pigs, the latter to represent the boars which long ago appeared at the *Jul* feast. *Pepparkakor* are made in various ways with the principal ingredients consisting of molasses, butter, light brown sugar, eggs, ginger and cinnamon, allspice, orange peel, cloves and flour.

Then, there are the dainty little cakes, called *klenater*, rich in egg yolks, butter, sugar, sifted flour and grated rind of lemon. These are fried by capable Swedish housewives in deep fat to a golden brown, after which they are drained on absorbent paper towels and dusted with powdered sugar.

CHRISTMAS CAKES AND PUDDINGS

Fruit Cake

1 cup butter
1 cup granulated sugar
1 cup brown sugar
4 eggs
1 teaspoon cloves
1 pound of raisins
1 pound of currants
½ pound citron

4½ cups flour
1 tablespoon cinnamon
1 teaspoon ginger
1 teaspoon nutmeg
1½ cups sour milk
1 tablespoon soda in 3 tbsp. hot coffee

Cream butter, add sugar and cream together well. Add beaten eggs. Dredge fruit and citron with flour. Sift flour and seasoning together. Add fruit and flour alternately with sour milk. Add soda dissolved in coffee. Mix.

Bake in two loaf tins in slow oven for 1½ to 2 hours.

Old-Fashioned Plum Pudding

3 eggs
½ pound raisins
½ pound currants
2 oz. citron (chopped)
1 pound flour (4 cups)

2 teaspoons nutmeg
½ teaspoon cinnamon
½ pound sugar
½ pound suet chopped fine
Milk—enough for stiff batter.

Separate yolks from whites of eggs. Dredge fruit and citron with flour. Combine dry ingredients. Add egg yolks and mix thoroughly, then add enough milk to make a stiff batter. Fold in beaten egg whites last. Turn into thickly floured square of unbleached cotton cloth, tie securely, leaving some space for pudding to swell, and plunge into boiling water. Boil gently five hours.

Use drawn butter and sugar sauce.

Frozen Rice and Apricot Pudding

½ cup rice
1 quart milk
1 cup sugar
4 eggs, separated
1 tablespoon lemon juice
1½ cups apricot pulp

Cook washed rice five minutes in boiling water. Drain and add to milk and one-half cup sugar in top of double boiler. Cook fifty minutes, covered. Add beaten egg yolks and cook five minutes longer. Cool. Whip egg whites, lemon juice, apricots and one-half cup sugar until mixture holds shape and fold into cooled rice, then freeze. This will yield 8 blocks—4 inches by 4 inches by one inch.

Gingerbread Cup Cakes

2 cups cake flour or
1¾ cups all-purpose flour
2 teaspoons baking powder
½ teaspoon salt
¼ teaspoon soda
2 teaspoons ginger
1 teaspoon cinnamon
⅓ cup shortening
⅓ cup sugar
⅔ cup honey
1 egg, well beaten
¾ cup sour milk or buttermilk

Sift dry ingredients together two or three times. Cream shortening, add sugar, honey and then egg and blend thoroughly. Add dry ingredients alternately with milk and beat thoroughly. Bake in a greased 9 x 9 inch pan or muffin tins in moderate oven (350° F.) 50 minutes (40 minutes for muffins). A delicious, feathery cake. Makes 16 cup cakes.

Yellow Angel Food Cake

5 eggs
½ cup cold water
1½ cups sugar
1½ cup flour
1 teaspoon baking powder
¼ teaspoon salt
1 teaspoon vanilla
¾ teaspoon cream tartar

Beat egg yolks until thick and lemon color. Add water and beat four minutes. Add sugar and beat another minute. Add flour, baking powder, and salt. Mix well with spoon but do not beat. Add vanilla. Beat the whites stiff, adding cream of tartar when foaming. Fold into batter and place in ungreased angel tube. Bake 15 minutes at low temperature of 275°. Then 325° another 30 or 35 minutes. Invert pans until cake is cold.

Mint Candy Cake

½ cup shortening	3 teaspoons baking powder
1¼ cups sugar	1 cup of milk
2⅓ cups flour	3 egg whites stiffly beaten
½ teaspoon salt	⅓ cup crushed peppermint candy

Cream shortening with sugar. Sift flour, measure, and sift with salt and baking powder. Add alternately with milk to first mixture. Mix thoroughly. Fold in stiffly beaten egg whites. Pour into well-greased cake pan. Bake in moderate oven (350° F.) 18 minutes. Cover top and sides of cake with icing, and if desired, sprinkle 1/3 cup crushed candy over cake while icing is moist.

Chocolate Surprise Cake

2 dozen lady fingers	4 egg yolks beaten light
½ pound cake sweet chocolate	1½ teaspoon vanilla
4 tablespoons sugar	4 egg whites beaten light
4 tablespoons water	1 cup whipped cream

Line pan with waxed paper. Line bottom and sides with lady fingers place browned side out. Melt chocolate. Add sugar, water, egg yolks. Cook until smooth, stirring constantly. Cool, then add vanilla and fold in egg whites. Pour half mixture into pan. Put another layer of lady fingers and add remainder of filling. Cover with waxed paper and place in refrigerator several hours. When ready to serve remove from pan and fill center with whipped cream. If so desired, sprinkle with chopped nuts and top with raspberries.

SEASONAL SALADS

Christmas Salad

1 package of lemon jello	1 small bottle of green cherries
1 small bottle of red cherries	1 small can of white grapes

Cut the cherries in half, and when the jello is partially firm, add the grapes and cherries and put the mixture in molds.

When firm place on lettuce leaves with mayonnaise and serve. Crackers and cheese could be served with this salad. If desired the cheese could be colored from the juice of the red and green cherries.

Frozen Fruit Salad

1 teaspoon gelatine	1 teaspoon sugar
2 tablespoons water	1 can fruit salad
1 cup of mayonnaise	1 banana
1 cup of whipped cream	

Soften gelatine and melt over stove. Combine with mayonnaise, cream and sugar and fold in fruit. Transfer to freezing tray and freeze three hours with cold control set at 5.

Pear Salad

Place the flat side of a half of sliced pear on a lettuce leaf and cover with cream cheese. Cut Tokay grapes in half and press them into the cream cheese to form a "bunch of grapes."

Ginger Ale Salad

- 1 package lemon jello
- ½ cup boiling water
- 1½ cups ginger ale
- 4 tablespoons nuts (finely chopped Optional)
- 4 tablespoons celery (finely chopped)
- 1 cup assorted fruits diced (pineapple-orange-apple-cherries-or grapes)

Dissolve jello in boiling water. Chill. Add ginger ale when slightly thickened, fold in nuts, celery, fruit. Turn into mold. For variation use only orange and grapefruit instead of assorted fruits and serve with watercress. (Optional.)

CHRISTMAS CANDIES

Divinity Fudge

- 1½ cups sugar
- ½ cup white Karo
- ¼ cup cold water
- 1 white egg
- 1 cup nuts

Stir sugar, Karo and water together and put on a low fire. Stir until all dissolved, cook same as boiled icing, only let it get harder, so it will hit against cup when put in cold water to test. Have the white of an egg, beaten stiff, and stir in the hot syrup, same as for boiled icing, only when all are stirred in, keep beating until the mixture cannot be beaten any longer, then stir in a cupful of nuts, the more the better. Put on butter-greased platter and cut in squares.

Vanilla Fondant

- 2 cups sugar
- 1 cup of water
- 1 tablespoon light corn syrup
- ¼ teaspoon glycerine
- 1 egg white
- 1 teaspoon vanilla

Put the sugar, water, and corn syrup into a saucepan and cook, stirring constantly over a low fire until the sugar is dissolved. Remove the spoon and do not stir the candy again during the cooking. When the candy begins to boil, add glycerine, cover the saucepan, and cook for three minutes. The steam formed, washes down any sugar crystals which may be thrown on the sides of the saucepan. Remove the cover and continue the cooking. Any sugar crystals which appear on the sides of the pan should be washed away with a fork covered with cheesecloth and dipped into cold water. Cook until 240 degrees F. is reached, pour at once on a cold, wet platter. Cool to 110 degrees F. (lukewarm) then beat the egg white until stiff and spread over the cooled fondant. Beat the mixture until the fondant becomes white and creamy.

Add vanilla and work until the mass is smooth and no lumps remain. Shape at once for centers and put in a cold place. This fondant softens upon standing, so that it should be dipped as soon as possible after shaping.

Peanut Brittle

1½ cups granulated sugar
1¾ cups dark corn syrup
⅔ cup cold water

½ pound blanched peanuts
1 tablespoon butter
¾ teaspoon soda

Boil sugar, syrup, water to hard-ball stage. Add peanuts and butter and stir hard until a brown color. Add soda dissolved in one teaspoon water. Mix well. Pour into well greased shallow pan. Break into pieces.

Walnut Cream Drops

1½ cups granulated sugar
1 cup milk
2 tablespoons white corn syrup
Pinch of salt

1 teaspoon vanilla extract
½ cup chopped Diamond Walnut kernels

Mix in a saucepan all ingredients except vanilla extract and Diamond Walnuts. Cook very slowly, without stirring, over a low heat to 236° F. or until a little of the mixture when dropped into cold water forms a soft ball. Remove from heat and cool at room temperature, without stirring, until lukewarm (145° F.). Add vanilla extract and Diamond Walnut kernels. Beat until candy holds its shape, then drop from teaspoon onto waxed paper. Makes about 20 patties.

Popcorn Balls

1 cup molasses
1 cup sugar
1 teaspoon of vinegar
2 tablespoons butter

¼ teaspoon baking soda
½ teaspoon of vanilla
4 quarts popped corn

Combine the molasses, sugar and vinegar. Boil and add the butter, soda and flavoring. Then pour into the popped corn, stirring rapidly. Rub the hands with butter and form the popcorn into balls.

A Delightful Temperance Drink

Christmas Punch

- 1 quart bottle grape juice
- 1 pint of lemon juice
- 1 pint of orange juice
- ½ pint of pineapple juice, or other sweet juice
- 1 bottle of carbonated water
- 1 pint of gingerale

Mix all ingredients and pour into punch bowl with block of ice. Cherries, sliced pineapple or oranges may be used as a garnish. This recipe will make about 2 gallons of punch.

CHAPTER V

CHRISTMAS CAROLS

WHEN THE heart is happy, the song is joyful. This is why carols are so appropriate for Christmas and no gathering during the festive season seems quite complete without raising voices in unison to the inspiring tunes and familiar words of the old favorites. In this chapter we have included the popular carols, known to everyone from childhood. They have a definite place in many of the programs suggested in the party section of this book. They are also to be used in connection with the presentation of the Christmas plays.

You have already read how the modern Christmas Carol originated in England and have perhaps noted that other countries have their Yuletide music, too. In Russia the old Kolyada songs to pagan deities, later dedicated to Christian saints, were sung in the streets up to the time of the Revolution. In France, the carols are known as Noël songs and in Germany the famous *Kristlieder* are heard wherever families or other groups congregate to enjoy Christmas music.

The very first Carol, in the opinion of many authorities, may be traced to St. Francis of Assisi, who made a crib resembling the manger bed of Jesus around which he and his brethren, and perhaps others, knelt while they sang of the Saviour's birth. Others go back even farther to the Bible, and say that this was the first carol ever sung: "Fear not: for, behold I bring you good tidings of great joy, which shall be to all people. For unto you is born this day in the city of David a Saviour, which is Christ the Lord. And this shall be a sign unto you; ye shall find the babe wrapped in swaddling clothes, lying in a manger... Glory to God in the highest, and on earth peace, good will toward men."

It is interesting to note the origin of the most widely sung Christmas carols. "Good King Wenceslas" is a recital of a legend referring to St. Wenceslas of Bohemia, translated by the Rev. Dr. Neale and sung to an old melody. "The Cradle Hymn" was written by Martin Luther for his children. That most inspiring carol, "Joy to the World" was penned by Dr. Isaac Watts. It is most commonly sung to the tune of "Antioch," from "The Messiah" by Handel.

Charles Wesley wrote "Hark! The Herald Angels Sing!" in 1739 and "Silent Night" was written by Joseph Mohr, Austria, and the music by Franz Gruber, another Austrian. "O Little Town of Bethlehem" was written by Rev. Phillips Brooks while he was rector of the Holy Trinity Church, Philadelphia. The hymn was set to music by Lewis H. Redner, a Philadelphia organist. The words and music of "We Three Kings of Orient Are" were created by Rev. John Henry Hopkins, D.D.

It is suggested that the carols be used at periodical intervals in the Christmas entertainment, and at the beginning and end of the plays. For home groups, the entire family will find them inspiring as they gather around the Christmas tree on the morning of the twenty-fifth to receive and to open their gifts. If you have slipped out of the habit of caroling on Christmas Eve, why not recapture one of the pleasant memories of youth this year by going from house to house singing greetings to the neighbors? At the close of the caroling, the groups in certain towns we know return to the church or school for a midnight lunch of coffee and cookies, a fitting climax to an invigorating custom of spreading good cheer.

CRADLE HYMN

IT CAME UPON THE MIDNIGHT CLEAR

Rev. Edmund H. Sears   (Carol.)   Richard S. Willis.

1. It came up-on the mid-night clear, That glo-rious song of old,
2. Still thro' the clo-ven skies they come, With peace-ful wings un-furled,
3. And ye, be-neath life's crush-ing load, Whose forms are bend-ing low,
4. For lo, the days are hast'n-ing on, By proph-et bards fore-told,

From an-gels bend-ing near the earth To touch their harps of gold:
And still their heaven-ly mu-sic floats O'er all the wea-ry world:
Who toil a-long the climb-ing way With pain-ful step and slow,—
When with the ev-er-cir-cling years Comes round the age of gold;

"Peace on the earth, good will to men, From heaven's all-gra-cious King."
A-bove its sad and low-ly plains They bend on hov-'ring wing,
Look up! For glad and gold-en hours Come swift-ly on the wing:
When peace shall o-ver all the earth Its an-cient splen-dors fling,

The world in sol-emn still-ness lay To hear the an-gels sing.
And ev-er o'er its Ba-bel sounds The bless-ed an-gels sing.
O rest be-side the wea-ry road And hear the an-gels sing.
And the whole world give back the song Which now the an-gels sing.

GOOD KING WENCESLAS

4 "Sire, the night is darker now,
  And the wind blows stronger;
Fails my heart, I know not how,
  I can go no longer."
"Mark my footsteps, my good page,
  Tread thou in them boldly:
Thou shalt find the winter's rage
  Freeze thy blood less coldly."

5 In his master's steps he trod,
  Where the snow lay dinted;
Heat was in the very sod
  Which the saint had printed;
Therefore, Christian men, be sure,
  Wealth or rank possessing,
Ye who now will bless the poor,
  Shall yourselves find blessing.

CHRISTMAS EVE

SONGS OF PRAISE THE ANGELS SANG

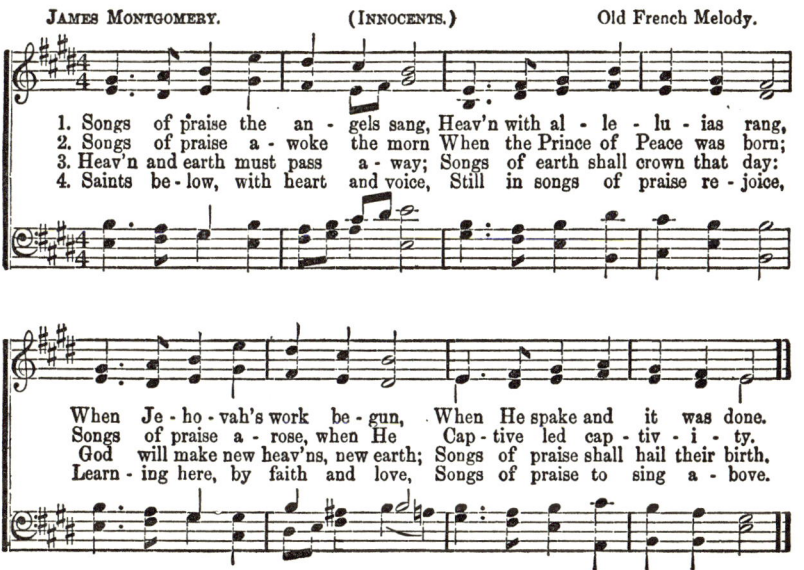

OH COME, ALL YE FAITHFUL

JOY TO THE WORLD

HARK! THE HERALD ANGELS SING

SILENT NIGHT

O LITTLE TOWN OF BETHLEHEM

WE THREE KINGS OF ORIENT

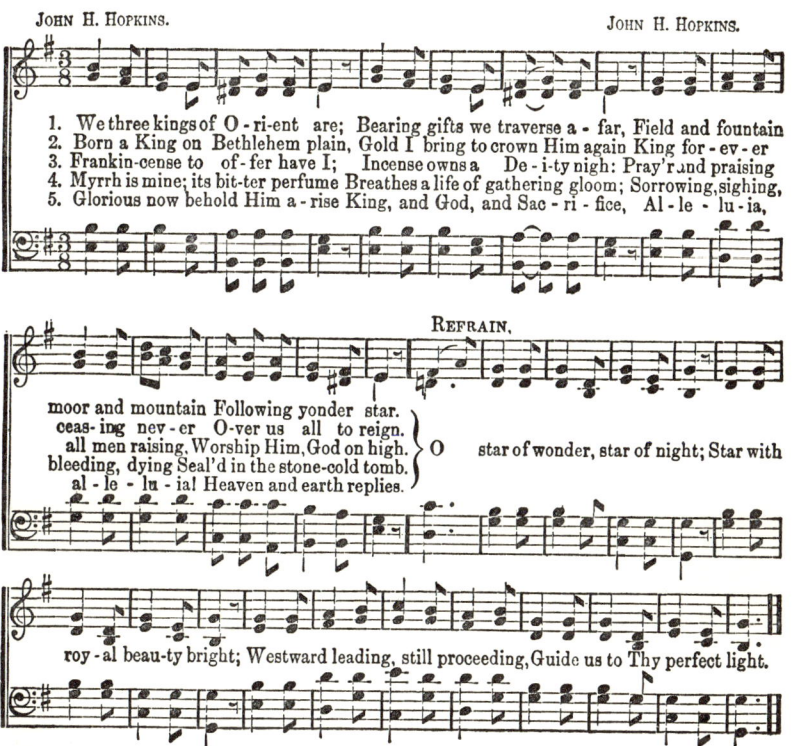

THE FIRST NOEL

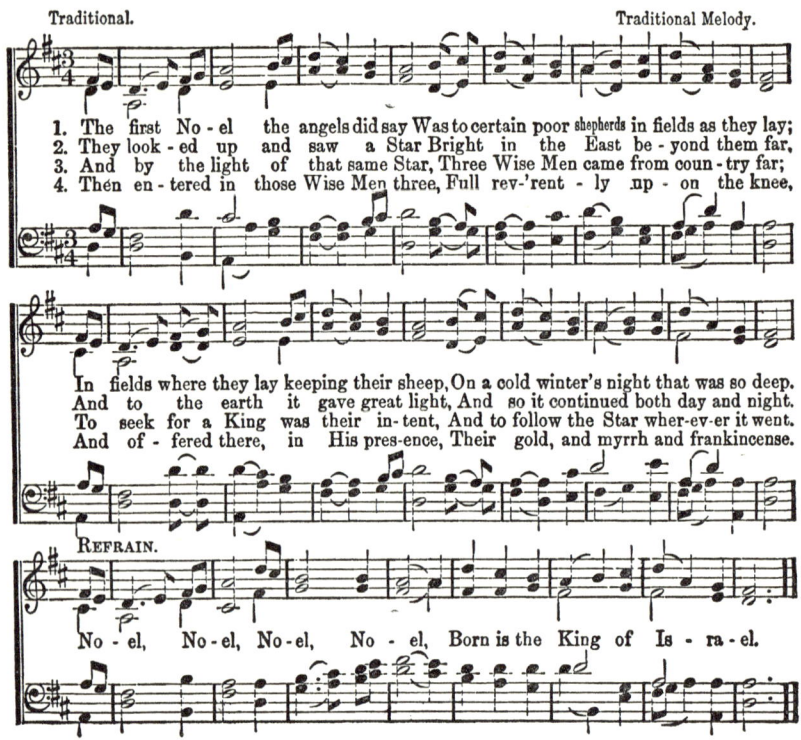

ONCE IN ROYAL DAVID'S CITY

5 And our eyes at last shall see Him
  Through His own redeeming love;
For that Child so dear and gentle
Is our Lord in heaven above;
And He leads His children on
To that place where He has gone.

6 Not in that poor lowly stable,
  With the oxen standing by,
We shall see Him; but in heaven
Set at God's right hand on high;
When like stars His children crowned,
All in white shall wait around.

GOD REST YOU MERRY, GENTLEMEN

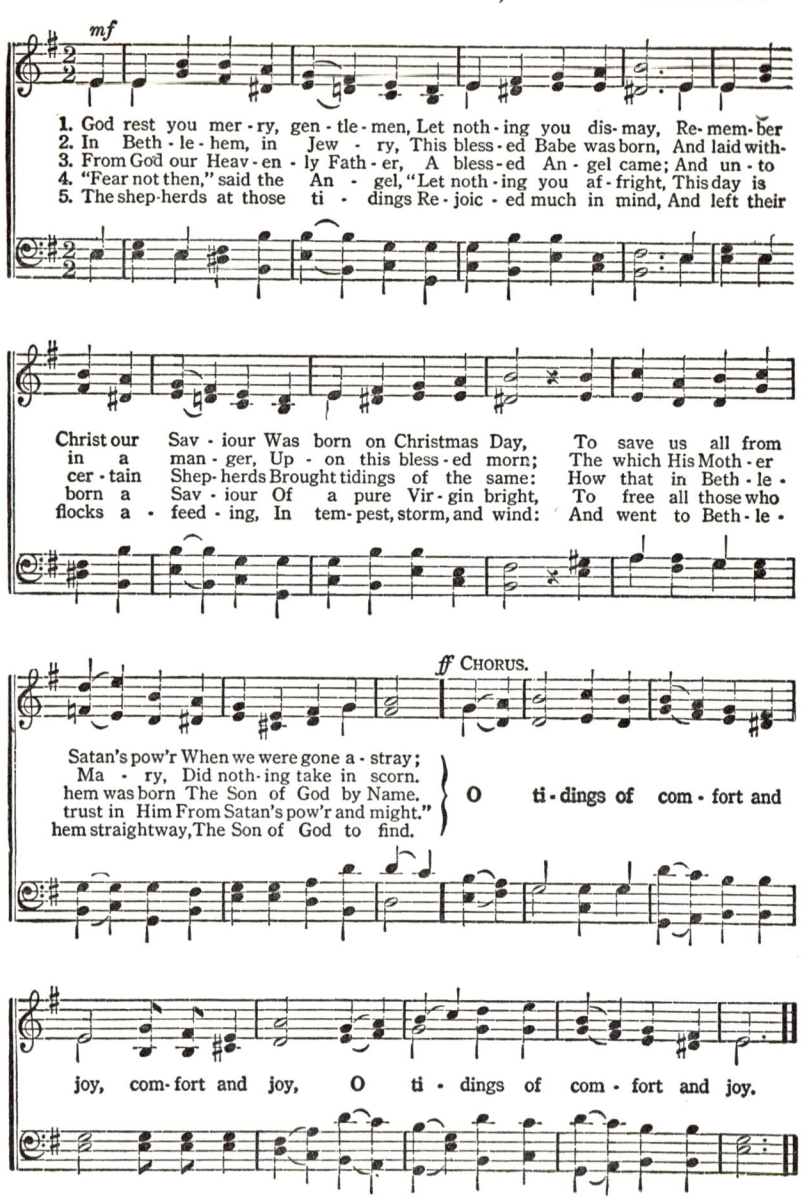

6 And when they came to Bethlehem
   Where our dear Saviour lay,
  They found Him in a manger,
   Where oxen feed on hay;
  His Mother Mary kneeling down,
   Unto the Lord did pray.

7 Now to the Lord sing praises,
   All you within this place,
  And with true love and brotherhood
   Each other now embrace;
  This holy tide of Christmas
   All other doth deface.

GOOD CHRISTIAN MEN, REJOICE

CHAPTER VI

CHRISTMAS PLAYS

WHETHER THESE plays are given for the enjoyment they will produce at the Christmas season or are presented as part of a program for raising funds for church or school class, the success or failure depends upon the way the affair is organized by the leader.

In coaching those who are taking an active part in a play or a series of recitations and skits, one must turn the actors into people who will live their parts, so to speak. So many presentations are spoiled by having the players move about on the platform like a bunch of wooden images. The leader should also remember to select capable assistants. When you try to do everything yourself, you will not have enough time free for coaching the play properly.

To accustom the players to move about naturally, it is better to rehearse on the stage or platform where the performance will be given, or use a room as nearly the same size and shape as possible. Never interrupt a rehearsal scene to give directions since this is apt to lead to confusion. Always do a scene as a whole, save your suggestions until it has ended, and then go over the entire scene again.

In order to emphasize the Christmas spirit manifested in these plays, you must thoroughly understand the play you direct. See it as a whole and remember please, your performers will be seen as well as heard. Have rehearsals enough so that the actions and dialogue go along smoothly.

The audience will enjoy singing a few Christmas carols before and after the staging of the shows. If there is a mixed audience, both plays might be given in the same afternoon or evening, the junior play to be followed by the senior production.

CHRISTMAS TREASURE
A short play for young people

CHARACTERS

MOTHER EDITH
RICHARD BOB
JEAN

SET: *The action takes place presumably in the living room of an average small family. However, no set or regular furniture need be employed. It may be given in a classroom, with the setting imagined.*

AT CURTAIN RISE: MOTHER *is sitting, with sewing or reading on her lap... She lifts her head as a door is slammed, then listens...*

MOTHER
Is that you, Richard?

RICHARD
(off stage)
Yes... Mother.

MOTHER
I'm in the living room...

RICHARD
(entering)
Hullo... (*yanks off cap and coat and tosses them aside, and sits near her*) It's getting cold. It'll snow, sure... tonight...

MOTHER
That will be fun, won't it? *(pause)* Where are the others?

RICHARD
Oh, they'll be home soon, I guess. I ran all the way... to get here first.

MOTHER
(smiling)
Hungry as usual? Or, hungrier... than usual?

RICHARD

I'm starving... as usual! But... (*eagerly*) more than that... I wanted to ask you something.

MOTHER

Oh! a secret?

RICHARD

Not exactly. It's more like a favor...

MOTHER

Yes—?

RICHARD

There are the best ice skates in the store window. And... well ... can I have them?

MOTHER

But... (*smiles with meaning*) if you did get them now... wouldn't you feel badly on Christmas morning, if there was no present for you?

RICHARD
(*hesitating*)

Well... (*pause—then quickly*) but... Christmas is ten days away. Anyway, Mother, if I had them now, I could get in a lot of skating, if it freezes....

MOTHER

We'll see about that, Richard. When the others come home, I'm going to tell you about a plan I have....

RICHARD

A plan—?

(*A door slams, off*)

MOTHER

Sh-sh! Here they come! (*turns to others as they troop in, little* JEAN *in the rear*) Hello, darlings... cold?

EDITH

Br—br! (*wiggles fingers in mitts*) I could use fur-lined gloves... and maybe a fur coat, and a bearskin cap like trappers wear and...

BOB
(*breaking in*)
It's going to snow, and if it piles deep on the hill...boy! that will be something...that is, it would be if I had skis....

MOTHER
(*laughing*)
Such children! You always want...something you don't have—! (*turns to talk to the assembled group en masse*) If Richard had skates, he'd want a bobsled! If Edith had fur-lined gloves, she'd want a fur muff. If Bob had skis...he'd get tired of them in no time at all and say that what he wanted most of all was another electric train! And Jean—here—what do you want more than anything else, Jean?

JEAN
(*the youngest and smallest*)
I...oh...about a million things...like, like...well, a doll, a stove, a set of dishes and...

EDITH
How about a pony?

JEAN
Oh, that would be nice, too. (*to* MOTHER) Is Santa going to bring all those things?

MOTHER
(*laughing*)
If Santa Claus were to bring this houseful of children everything *they think they want*, he'd have to hire all the express trucks and freight cars and airplanes in the world...no single little sleigh would do! (*pause*) And that's why...I've got a plan for all of you.

CHORUS
Plan—? What kind of plan—?

MOTHER
I think you are all old enough to learn the value of money. You ask for things, get them, and forget them. You never count the cost....

JEAN
(*trembling voice*)
Is this... a scolding, Mother? Were we... naughty?

MOTHER
No, just thoughtless.

RICHARD
But... what's the plan?

MOTHER
Christmas is only a few days away. And this Christmas each of you is to be your own Santa Claus....

JEAN
(*frightened*)
You mean... Santa won't come to our house? (*is close to tears*) But I want him to! I want him to!

MOTHER
Sh, Jean. Santa will be here, just as he is every Christmas. No one can keep him away, for he's the spirit of Christmas... only this time, he's going to expect you to help him make you all happy.

EDITH
I don't understand, Mother, what do you mean?

MOTHER
This Christmas Santa will trim our tree, as he always does. But each of you must decide what you want most of all, and buy it for yourself....

RICHARD
Buy what we want?

MOTHER
No one knows the cost of anything... big or small, until he has to pay for it.

BOB
(*frowning*)
But to pay for something, you've got to have money....

MOTHER

Not always... there are things that money can't buy. Things you get to own—and love—that you can't see or touch or smell or hear or even taste... but that become part of you, after you've spent some of yourself to pay for it! But... that's too deep for you, isn't it?

RICHARD

Well... I don't exactly see what it's got to do with ice skates!

MOTHER

Some day you will! (*laughs*) But now it's enough if you learn to appreciate the ice skates, after you've spent your own money to get them!

RICHARD

My own money—? But, I don't have any—

MOTHER

That is my plan. Each of you is to have some money.

CHORUS

But—how?

MOTHER

Today I will give each of you an envelope. In each is the same amount of money. You must buy what you want—what you truly believe you want most—and not ask me, or your father... or... (*smiles at* JEAN) Santa Claus for a single other thing! Now, do you understand?

RICHARD

That's a great idea. Now I can get *exactly what* I want!

EDITH

I like your plan, too, Mother.

MOTHER

Each month, you will get an envelope, just like the one today. You must learn to manage and spend wisely what you get, because it will be all you will have for a whole month....

BOB

Gosh...! Money every month! Gosh—!

MOTHER
You'll make mistakes. Spend it on things you *think* you want, and then realize you don't have any left for something you *really* want or need. But that is the only way you can learn.

RICHARD
I won't make any mistakes. I know *exactly* what I want.

MOTHER
(*smiling, as she goes to table or desk for envelopes and distributes them*)

Well... we will see how it works out. Here is your first money. And your first lesson in learning values! (*each child clutches his or her envelope, with shining face*) Remember! (*she smiles at them*) When this is gone, you can't ask for more, or for anything you want... for a whole month!

EDITH
Oh, we'll remember... Mother!

(*Exit* MOTHER)

BOB
Real money. (*touches envelope happily*) Real money to spend!

JEAN
I know what I am going to buy.

RICHARD
Shoes!

JEAN
(*shaking head*)

No.

EDITH
(*pointing to* JEAN's *shoes*)

But you need a new pair.

BOB
She always does. That's because she's always scuffing and scraping her feet. And that's because she's a baby....

JEAN
I'm not a baby! I'm not...!

RICHARD
(*to her*)
Mother is right... absolutely. If you have to pay for your shoes, you'll be more careful of them.

JEAN
I'm not going to buy shoes! (*runs off, and exit*)

EDITH
(*to the boys*)
Why do you tease her? She's... such a little thing.

BOB
She shouldn't get as much as we do, because she'll do foolish things with her money... buy lollipops... or something like that ...ugh! she's always leaving them... all sticky... on chairs and places, and I sit on 'em....

RICHARD
Say... for that matter... who put chewing gum on the window seat?

BOB
All right, all right...! Let it go...!

EDITH
Now, let me see... should I buy the gloves... or a nice, soft muff....

RICHARD
Better be sure which you want more.

EDITH
The gloves would be more sensible. Still... one of those muffs with a purse in them... that would be dressy, kind of—

BOB
(*putting hands to ears*)
Spare us the style points.

RICHARD

We've got our own problems...

BOB

Now that I think about it, I'm not so sure I do know what I want. What are you going to buy, Ritchie?

RICHARD

A pair of skates.

BOB

The ones in the window of Brown Brothers? That's a good pair, all right. (*pause*) Say, suppose I do get skis... and you, skates... could we kind of swap them sometimes?

RICHARD

Take turns using them? Say! That *is* a good idea!

EDITH

The gloves? *No*, the muff. Oh, I wish I knew which I want more!

BOB

Why don't you just get another doll?

EDITH

(*drawing herself up*)
I've outgrown dolls. I'm not Jean.

RICHARD

You're worse than she is. At least, she knew what she wanted.

EDITH

And... I suppose, all this arguing you've been doing with Bob means you do, too?

BOB

We weren't arguing. We were settling our affairs....

EDITH

Oh, indeed?
(JEAN *returns with a heavy package, bulkily wrapped*)

RICHARD

For goodness sake! Look at Jean.

EDITH
(*turning to her*)

Whatever is that, Jean?

JEAN
(*defiantly*)

It's not shoes.

BOB

I hope not...! Your feet aren't *that* big!

RICHARD

Shame on you, Jean. You needed new shoes and you bought something else.

EDITH

Something foolish, I'll wager!

BOB

You're such a baby!

JEAN

I'm not a baby. (*has put down package to floor, and stamps feet*) And what I bought isn't foolish....

BOB

You've got to admit whatever it is... (*walks around package, looking at it*) It's a foolish shape. A mighty, mighty foolish shape!

JEAN
(*almost crying*)

It is not! It's beautiful... awful beautiful!

EDITH

Oh, let her alone. She'll learn. It's her money, isn't it?

BOB
(*touching package with an exploratory finger*)

But what is it? (*looks at* JEAN) Another doll?

JEAN

No!

RICHARD

Did it cost all your money?

JEAN
(*nods*)

Yes.

BOB

See? What'd I tell you? She spent all of her money at one time, buying something she didn't need!

EDITH

(*kneeling and unwrapping package while* JEAN *looks alternately tearful and frightened*)
Well, we'll just find out what it is... no sense to scold her until we know what she bought! (*The package opened reveals a poinsettia plant, tied with a red ribbon.*—EDITH *exclaims... sitting back in astonishment.* BOB *whistles softly.*)

RICHARD

It is beautiful, Jean. It's like you said, awful beautiful. But, what are you going to do with a plant?

BOB

You can't even eat it!

JEAN

It's for Mother. It's her Christmas present.
Subdued CHORUS

Oh.

JEAN

Mother likes flowers. And she likes Christmas. And the man in the store said this was a Christmas flower. And it's not foolish at all... (*in a rush*) it will *keep* and stay beautiful, the man said it would, for a long time!

BOB

That is right, all that the man told you, Jean. It *is* a Christmas flower... why nearly all Christmas cards are decorated with poinsettias!

JEAN

Mother said we were to buy what we wanted most, and that's what I wanted most... to buy something for her.

EDITH

I feel *so* ashamed! And selfish!

RICHARD

So do I.

BOB

Maybe, Jean's not very practical. But she's the best of us all... (*to* JEAN) I'm sorry I called you a baby.

EDITH

Poor little Jean. Spending all her money *to give* something, when she really *needed* shoes!

JEAN
(*anxiously*)

Do you think Mother will like the flower?

RICHARD

Like it? She'll love it!

EDITH

I don't really need gloves, I've got mitts. And a muff is kind of silly.... I couldn't carry much stuff if I had a muff to carry, too—

RICHARD

My old skates aren't so bad, if I'd clean and sharpen them—

BOB

Listen! Let's *all* give Mother that plant!

EDITH

That wouldn't be fair! Jean paid for it... and thought it up! (*She looks at* JEAN's *shoes and continues*) *Her* shoes are shabby and scuffed terribly.

BOB

What I meant was we'd all give Jean some of our money, so that we'd each have an interest in the poinsettia. Then, it would be to Mother from all of us—see?

RICHARD

And Jean can get shoes with what we give her!

BOB

Sure!—

EDITH

(*Jumping up*)

And we'd still have money enough left over to buy other **things!** Oh... (*claps hands*) I've got the grandest idea... (*closes eyes and pauses*)

RICHARD

What is it? Don't go into a trance! Tell us what the idea is!

EDITH

(*opening eyes*)

We could get Grandmother a warm wool scarf, Aunt Mary some nice handkerchiefs,—

RICHARD

(*breaking in*)

And Dad that fishing magazine he's always talking about!

BOB

I'm with you! That's exactly what we'll do!

RICHARD

But, say... will we have money enough to buy something for everybody?

EDITH

We'll all go to my room, right now... (*swoops up plant and paper*) and make out a list... and you, Richard, you're the best in arithmetic... you can add it all up and see how much it will cost!

JEAN

(*jumping up and down*)

I'm so excited!

EDITH

We all are!

JEAN

I'm all tingly... up and down my back!

EDITH
(*laughing*)
That's the Christmas spirit, Jean... and you're full of it. I feel kind of tingly myself....

RICHARD
And so do I!

BOB
This is better than owning the best skis in the whole world! (*pause, then, running for door*) Let's go! (ALL *follow him*)

RICHARD
'Ray...'ray for Christmas!

CHORUS
'Ray...'ray for Christmas! (*Exeunt*)

(*Curtain*)

REUNION AT CHRISTMAS

A Play: One—Act:

Curtain for Time—

SET: *One Interior: The living room of an average family on the outskirts of a typical small farming community town.*

Furniture in fashion a generation ago. Stiffly upholstered chairs, sofas, etc.... pictures and family portraits on walls. Lace curtains at windows. Lace doilies on tables, lace chair backs on chairs and sofa.

Back-stage, one broad window or two smaller, high ones.

Left-stage, door to vestibule or hall, leading to front porch.

Right-stage, portiered doorway leading to other parts of house.

Because it is Christmas Eve, holly wreaths are at the windows; if a fireplace is used, it is trimmed with holly, too, and hung on its mantel are stockings for eight, already bulging and filled.

Holly or other trims in vases, behind pictures, etc.

Center-rear, between two windows, or slightly beyond the one if only one is made, is a tall Christmas tree, nearly trimmed, and a step-ladder, with a litter of boxes, tissues, etc. on floor.

Gaily wrapped gift-boxes are piled near fireplace or on sofa, chairs, floor—etc.

CHARACTERS

ADA MARTIN:	*Talkative, successful business woman, widow of John Martin. Dresses in smart, matronly manner ...a bit tailored.*
JACK MARTIN:	*Her son, awkward but not unattractive youth, about nineteen.*
NEALE MARTIN:	*Eldest son of the family, about forty-five, built on the plump side.*
SALLY MARTIN:	*His pretty daughter, about seventeen.*
LAURA MARTIN:	*Wife of Neale, mother of Sally, very much a home-woman, comfortably frilly in her clothes and manner...fortyish.*
DORA:	*Maid of all work. One of those "treasures", though badly trained and uniform-less.*

CORINNE: *The only senior Martin daughter, younger than her brothers, brittle and gay in manner, smart and sophisticated in her choice of clothes, and appearing much younger than she is.*
ROY MARTIN: *The returned black-sheep. Flashy and loud-voiced and more than a bit sarcastic in the beginning, his "show-off" manners quickly disappear.*
GRANDMOTHER MARTIN, *around whom the entire play is built and who is talked about, but never seen.*

AT CURTAIN RISE:—NEALE *is on ladder putting ornaments on tree, which is practically trimmed. He is in shirt and trousers with bright suspenders, and his collar is unfastened and his sleeves rolled.*

There is a disordered pile of emptied boxes and tissue paper at bottom of tree, and ADA *is handing trims to* NEALE. SALLY *stands at window, staring out.* JACK *is sprawled in a chair, front—apparently supposed to string pink and white popcorn, but in reality eating more than he strings—he is in trousers, sports shirt and very loud sweater.*

Throughout action JACK *eats the popcorn, the few lines he says punctuated by swallows and lusty chewing of it, until* ADA *stops him... thereafter, until the popcorn adorns the tree... he surreptitiously snitches a bite from time to time.*

At first, there is silence... NEALE *industriously putting on balls, etc. on tree, and* ADA *studying effect, standing off and squinting at tree....*

JACK *chewing and half-humming.* SALLY *tapping her fingers nervously on sill.... Then—*

ADA

Neale! (*startled, he turns precariously on ladder*) I think this red one, maybe... at the top... (*hands it to him*) and take down the green... we've got two greens.... (*he takes off a green, holds it, puts on red*) No... (*sighs*) that's not much better! It's hopeless

...trying to get any kind of artistic effect.... (*stands off, staring at tree*) Maybe if you moved that blue thing...it looks like a kind of Jack in a box...yes... (*pointing as* NEALE *tries to locate the trim she means*) that one... (*sighs again*) we've got a red...a green...and...oh! now, there are two reds together, aren't there? Take it off...will you? Yes—that red one! (NEALE *is now holding the green, the blue and the last red trim*)

JACK
(*swallowing hastily*)
There's no use making Uncle Neale work like a dog....

ADA
(*snappishly*)
Who's making your Uncle Neale work like a dog? For heavens' sake we all want a nice tree, don't we?

JACK
The worse it looks...the more helter skelter the effect, the better Grandmother Martin will like it....

ADA
Nonsense! Just because all we've got are the same trims we've had for the last twenty years is no reason to just *throw* them on the tree....

JACK
(*plopping another piece of popcorn into his mouth*)
That's how Grandmother likes 'em...just thrown on....

ADA
(*ignoring him and turning to* NEALE)
Now, at the store, we've got the grandest tree. A tree that is a Christmas tree. You know...modern. It's in the window...and it's all white. A snow and frost effect. Just white. That's all. Except for small concealed blue lights, they're tucked under the branches and don't show until it's lit up...and...well... (*sighs*) when that tree's lit...well...that's a tree that *is* a Christmas tree....

NEALE

(*who has wearily seated himself on top of ladder during all of this, still holding the three trims in dispute*)
Where'll I put these?

ADA

Oh... (*stands off, and right into a box, looks down in dismay*) dear... dear! What have I done? (*stoops and picks up a smashed silver trim*) Why—it's that funny little silver star... you know, the one Grandmother bought the last year Grandpa was alive... oh, dear! do you think we could glue it together...? Make it stick somehow? (*looks pleadingly at* NEALE) You know how Grandmother Martin is... she never forgets a single trim! Looks for them... points them out to us... tells us all about each and every one, she's been doing that for ten—twelve, maybe twenty Christmases—and now... this star... the one that she put on the tree herself the last year Grandpa was alive! (LAURA *enters from right, and* ADA *turns to her tragically—*)

LAURA

(*briskly*)
I greased her chest... she's sleeping like a child... land sakes, Ada... what've you got there? ... you're holding it like it's a newly hatched egg!

ADA

(*very tragically*)
It's the silver star. You know, the one Grandmother Martin has had ever since the last Christmas Grandpa was alive... and I've... I've *broken* it!

LAURA

Oh... that's the trouble with having a Christmas tree here. It just reeks with sentiment. Every single ball, every bit of tinsel... everything... is packed full of memories for her!

ADA

I know....

LAURA
(*going to her and peering at the damage*)
Maybe we could kind of ... mend it. ...

NEALE
(*loudly but resignedly*)
What'll I do with these?

LAURA
(*looking at him*)
Land sakes, Neale! Aren't you through with that tree, yet? (*He just about collapses on ladder ... when ...*)

SALLY
(*excited*)
Here comes Corinne...!
General gasp and CHORUS
Corinne?

SALLY
She's getting out of a cab ... she's coming up the drive. ...

LAURA
What's her new fiancé look like? Is he ... (*she runs for window*) tall?

SALLY
She's alone. ...

ADA
(*joining* SALLY *and* LAURA)
Alone—?

SALLY
She's got a lot of bundles. ...

LAURA
(*nose pressed to window*)
It's so dark... I can hardly see her... are you sure it's Corinne? I was beginning to think she'd not get here at all!

ADA
Yes... that's Corinne... who else could it be? But for heaven's sake... where's that boy friend of hers? I was dying to meet him.... (JACK *is up, too, and at the window, chewing like mad.* NEALE *sits... resignedly on ladder—*)

LAURA
It's about time we did get to meet one of her beaux. She never stays with one to last through Christmas... what a mean disposition she has!

NEALE
Where'll I put these? (*gestures with trims he holds*)

ADA
Quick! She's on the porch... get Dora... (*runs back toward right, shouting*) Dora! Dora! (*Bell rings—*DORA *comes on from right, tying apron about her.... She is wearing a house dress and her apron is a "cover-all"—she is the repressed, overworked... "hired girl" type*)

DORA
(*talking as she enters and moves to door*)
I'm coming... for Pete's sake, can't anyone open doors around but me? (ALL *stand around now—a little welcoming group. Except* NEALE....)

NEALE
(*in a last feeble attempt*)
Where will I put these? (*He is ignored by the welcoming committee who fairly "rush"* CORINNE *when* DORA *opens door... and in standing to peer over their heads, he nearly topples and in reaching out into space to catch his balance, down go the red, the green and the blue balls to floor. He stares at them for a moment, then sits on the ladder... as....*)

CORINNE
(*gaily entering, fur-coated and laden with packages*)
Merry Christmas, Dora....

DORA
Same to you, Miss Corinne....

CORINNE
(*dumping packages into* DORA'S *arms*)
Merry... Yuletide... all! (*babble of greetings all at once—*)
Merry Christmas! Greetings! Hi–! You're looking grand!

CORINNE *is kissed in turn by* ADA, LAURA, SALLY... *and awkwardly, only after she's put her face up for it, by* JACK....

She advances into room, others thinning out about her so that all may be seen to advantage—

SALLY *takes* CORINNE'S *coat, hat and bag and puts them on a chair or sofa....*

DORA *deposits the boxes with other boxes, stands for a moment arms a-kimbo surveying room, occupants three... then with a sniff, strides off, right....*

CORINNE
(*talking in gay little gasps*)
A ghastly ride all the way from New York. Snow... hail... ugh! (*shivers*) but here... safe at home... at last! (*laughs*) Where's Neale? (*sees him, waves*) Hi, darling! (*throws him a kiss*) And where's Grandmother Martin?

JACK *goes back to his popcorn munching and stringing—*

LAURA
She had a little cold. I greased her chest, and put her to bed....

CORINNE

I'll run up and say hello to her.... (*starts right*)

ADA

She's taking a nap, Corry....

CORINNE

Then... it's nothing serious?

LAURA

No... she's a bit tuckered out, that's all... (*smiles arching her brows*) too much Christmas excitement. She's such a child about it, never grows old!

CORINNE

I... I know.... (*walks to table, fiddles about with objects on it*)

ADA

You just sit down somewhere, Corinne... you must be tired out, too... that long ride! And the snow! (*sits, holding silver star guiltily and carefully*) Dora'll give you something hot to drink in a little while....

LAURA

(*going to boxes*)
I'll straighten these! Land sakes!—look at the heap of them! Such pretty wrappings as you use, Corry... can always tell your presents. I hate to open 'em... seems a shame to rip those fancy fixin's apart... (*picks up a box and peers at it*) For Grandmother Martin! (*shakes it*) What is it... a shawl?

NEALE *giving up all hope of help is scrambling up and down ladder putting on last of the trims any old way....*
SALLY *is sitting on sofa's arm. Studying* CORINNE....
CORINNE *turns....*

CORINNE

Well... why don't you ask me what you really want to? (*They stare uncomfortably at her, suspending their various activities....*) Ever since, I've come into this room, you've wanted to... ask me about... Bill, haven't you? But you've been afraid to... or maybe, too tactful....

NEALE

(*turning on ladder, and breaking into the uneasy pause*)
All right, Corry... I'll ask you... where is that new friend of yours?

CORINNE

Bill... (*squares shoulders and tilts up chin*) couldn't come ... he's sailed to... to South America. Rio.

ADA

South America—?

CORINNE

Very unexpectedly. A big business deal. (*starts walking down, then to tree, talking as she moves*) He's busy, you know, terribly busy. One of those big, big, important men. Always getting calls to go here and there, to attend to this and that.... (*laughs gaily*) You'd think there was only one Mr. Fix-it in the world! (*waves her hand gracefully*) Most annoying, of course... and upsetting... but what can I do?

JACK

(*bluntly*)
Why didn't you go with him?

CORINNE

(*after a little pause*)
Oh... (*almost too smoothly*) I wouldn't miss Christmas at home! Not... not for anything! (*abruptly as she reaches ladder*) Let me help, will you, Neale? You don't know how I've been looking forward to this tree! Did you leave a space... for me to fill? 'Way... way up high?

NEALE
Sure...sure...! (*turns to her and speaks gently*) This time ...I mean...this Bill of yours and the way you feel about him ...is different, isn't it, Corry?

CORINNE
Well.... (*laughs*) How did you know?

NEALE
You've not spouted off any of your usual bright sayings... about love being a mirage...and stuff like that....

CORINNE
Oh... (*laughs again*) but that's no guarantee, darling...that I won't. The evening's young.... (*picks up one of the few remaining trims*) And now...how about this...? Next to the silver one?

ADA
(*plaintively, looking at silver star in her hands*)
I wish I knew what to do with this. It's like a blot on my conscience. It'll spoil my whole Christmas...I know....

DORA *appears suddenly at door ...crosses to window carrying a lighted candle in a hurricane lamp and puts it on sill.... All mechanically move to make way for her. She turns and recrosses to door. Does not speak nor do they until she reaches door right....*

DORA
'Taint as big a candle as usual. I used it up some yesterday, when the fuses burnt out....(*Exit*)

CORINNE
(*laughingly waving a graceful hand*)
Everything's just the same, isn't it? Everything just goes on ...like we do! Even that!... (*points to candle*) The old familiar ritual!...

LAURA

I've got such a funny feeling... excited like. Wouldn't it be funny... if Roy did come back this Christmas?

SALLY

You had the same funny feeling last Christmas—and the Christmas before that... and Uncle Roy's not back yet!

CORINNE *narrows her eyes and looks at* SALLY—

NEALE

If—and when—he does come home I'm going to ask him right off for that five dollars he borrowed!

SALLY
(*impatiently*)
Oh, can't you forget that darned old five dollars?

NEALE

Well, I tell you five dollars was a lot of money... to me then. I had to work a week to earn it. Thought I was lucky at that!

LAURA

It was twenty-nine years, come midnight, that Roy just walked out of that front door....

SALLY

You were trimming the tree, just like now. He went after more tinsel to put on it....

LAURA

Why, pet... how do you know?

SALLY

I've heard it often enough‘

LAURA

Oh. Well, he went right out of that front door, and he never came back.

SALLY
Why should he come back?

ADA
Sally—!

LAURA *has gone back to sorting and re-piling the unopened gift boxes.*

LAURA
And him... Roy, no more than fifteen at the time! That would make him... let's see... (*counts rapidly on fingers*) forty-four! Land sakes! How time flies. (*goes back to boxes*)

CORINNE
I don't remember Roy very well. I was so much younger than the boys. Only a baby...

ADA
(*straightening a holly trim*)
You were ten years old....

CORINNE
(*hastily*)
But I do remember every Christmas... there's always been a candle in the window, just like tonight, to light him home. Rather pretty, at that, isn't it? Grandmother Martin's faith, I mean, that Roy will return some Christmas night....

JACK
(*suddenly*)
Maybe he's never been able to come... because he's been in jail!

ADA
(*sharply*)
Jack Martin! He's your uncle! Your own father's brother.... (*suddenly noticing what he had been doing to the popcorn*) Jack! That corn's to be strung... not eaten! Stop it this minute... the eating, I mean... and get busy on stringing it... a white, a pink

...and so on! First thing you know, Grandmother'll be down, and the tree not even ready....

JACK

Aw, gee...Mom...I feel like a sissy...doing this...why don't Sally do it?

ADA

Sally will help, won't you (*turning to* SALLY) dear?

SALLY

(*not very graciously*)
Oh, I guess so. Nothing changes in this family. Nothing. Not even Jack—he's the perennial infant!

JACK

Say—you don't have to act like a sore-head...just because you couldn't go to some fool party....

SALLY

(*stamping her feet at him*)
It was not a fool party. It was the party of the year! But then you wouldn't know anything about anything like that! You're nothing but...a...a popcorn-eating gourmet!

NEALE

(*from his position of placing a trim*)
The word, Sally, is gourmand.

JACK

(*angrily to* SALLY)
Say! If this Romeo was as crazy about you...as...you'd like to believe he was...why didn't he come here with you? Answer me that.... (*plops another piece of popcorn into his mouth*) If you can!

SALLY

(*furiously*)
Oh...you...! (*scathingly*) Maybe...I didn't want him to meet you...to know I had such an imbecile for a cousin!

ADA
(*who has now gone to tree turns and sees* JACK *at the popcorn again*)
Jack! That corn's to be strung!

SALLY
(*running to* CORINNE)
Aunt Corinne!

CORINNE
Yes—?

SALLY
Is he handsome—I mean—is Bill handsome?

CORINNE
(*slowly*)
Yes. Very handsome.

SALLY
Is... is he romantic? You know... dashing... and tall and young?

CORINNE
Yes (*swallows*) (*smiles*) but why this catechism? We've... (*turns back to* NEALE) got a tree to trim!

SALLY
Oh, bother the tree. You don't care about it, really. Not more than we do!

LAURA
Sally!

SALLY
(*persisting to* CORINNE)
Do things happen to him? You know—exciting, thrilling, *alive* things?

CORINNE
Why... why... yes... I guess things do happen to Bill. He's ... he's that kind.

SALLY
(*positively*)
I knew it. I just knew that....

LAURA
(*louder*)
Sally!

SALLY
We... we just go on doing the same old things over and over again. Saying the same old things over and over again. Even hoping the same old things over and over again. Christmas after Christmas... oh, I'm sick of it!

LAURA
(*louder*)
Sally! Sally Martin!

SALLY
Don't you see how silly we are? How... ordinary? So awfully ordinary, we're not even interesting to each other! We're deadly dull... That's why Aunt Corinne didn't bring Bill here. She didn't want to disillusion him... have him see her with such a *dead* family stifling her! I'll bet... yes, I'll just bet... he didn't go off to South America... or anywhere! (*so wound up she can't stop*) We don't want to come here. We don't care, really, if we *never* see each other. We just pretend we care. It's a Christmas habit, that's all it is! We'd all rather be somewhere else... be with somebody else... but we keep on pretending... because we think it's our duty. Our duty to the family, to Grandmother Martin... and I'll bet if the truth were known, she's as bored with the whole thing as we are! As bored with us... as we are with each other! I'm... I'm... sick of it. Sick... and... (*wails, turning to door, right*) tired of... nothing happening! (*Exit on a run*)

ADA
Well...! (*goes to cartons by tree*) I was never so insulted in my life. I'm boring... am I? (*drops silver star down into tissues, etc.*) Rubbish! (*to all of them*) I'll have you understand, I'm no Martin! I only... married one!

CORINNE
I ... I envy Sally!

ADA
You envy her? (*laughs shrilly*) what she needs, big as she thinks she is ... is a good spanking!

CORINNE
She's so young. So terribly young. She can still *feel* ... things.
(DORA *enters abruptly, dust pan and brush in hand* ...

ADA
That is no excuse for bad manners ... other have feelings, too ... (*exit grandly*)

DORA
I put coffee and sandwiches on the kitchen table. There's two kinds of cake, too ... (*pause*) Go and get it ... (*starts in straightening room*)

JACK
(*leaping to his feet*)
Yippee! Is there a chocolate cake, Dora?

DORA
Yep. White icing.

JACK
Boy! I'm starved ... (*exit on a run*)

LAURA
(*wringing her hands*)
Oh ... dear! My Christmas spirits ... are wilted ... completely wilted ... (*exit*)

CORINNE
(*going to door*)
Coming, Neale? ... (*turns to Dora*) Where is the 'phone, Dora?

DORA

Same old place. In the hall... (*Corinne exit—frowning*)

NEALE

(*scrambling down from ladder laboriously panting*)
Not much in the way of lively Christmas spirits around...

DORA

(*going on with her work*)
This is not a drinking family...

NEALE

Never took a drink in my life. Maybe... that's what's the mattei with me... (*pause, as Dora looks at him, startled, then he goes on*). Did you say... there was cold, sliced ham, Dora?

DORA

I didn't say. But there is... as usual. And sweet pickles. And Swiss cheese. The holey-kind—

NEALE

That's great... (*starts, right, stops, turns*) Oh... I say, Dora... (*guiltily*) I didn't quite finish the tree. There are a couple of things left over... and... er... er... we... broke... that is, a thing or two broke... you know, went to pieces on us... too old, I guess.

DORA

(*sighing*)
That's all right... Mr. Neale. I'll finish the tree. I'll sweep up the trash so there won't be a piece left... and I'll (*looks at popcorn string*) finish the corn stringing. You just run along and have your coffee...

NEALE

Thanks, Dora... thank... (*exit in haste*)

DORA *sighs . . . sits down and starts in stringing—*
Someone taps on window from outside. Startled, she gets up,

stares, hand to mouth . . . then, quickly, runs to door, left and opens it—
A man in a loud overcoat with a bright muffler about his neck comes in, depositing a bag on the floor and looking around . . . he is big . . . rather flashy . . .

ROY

It's . . . all as it was. Just the same . . . (*to Dora*) except you. Who are you—?

DORA

I . . . I am Dora. The help . . .

ROY

Oh . . . (*he touches a chair softly*) Oh. Just the same. Everything the same . . .

DORA goes to window and blows out candle . . .

Why did you do that, Dora?

DORA
(*turning*)
You're home . . . it's done its duty . . .

ROY

You know who I am?

DORA

You're . . . the one that ran off. You're Roy Martin.

ROY

Yes . . .

DORA

She'll be glad . . . she's waited for you . . .

ROY

I was afraid to ask . . . afraid maybe . . . she wasn't around any longer . . .

DORA

Grandmother Martin is alive and hearty... she's upstairs... I'll get her...

ROY

No... no, not just yet. Who else... of the family is here?

DORA

Neale and his wife, Laura... and their girl, Sally...

ROY

They have a girl?

DORA

Seventeen, she is. Miss Corinne's here, too...

ROY

Corry never married? She was a pretty bit...

DORA

Well, she's always going to be married—off an' on... collects boy friends but her temper and temper'ment are more than they can stand.

ROY

Oh. And John—?

DORA

He's been dead for five years.

ROY

Dead! John dead!—

DORA

His widow's here... Ada... and her boy, Jack...

ROY

Well... well... time does go on, doesn't it, Dora?

DORA

Not very fast around here....

ROY
It... it never did. That's why... I ran off...

DORA
I... hope you brought some tinsel.

ROY
Tinsel—? (*then, laughing and putting his hand into pocket*) I did... (*draws out a bolt of bright tinsel*) and here it is!

DORA
(*taking it and holding it to her breast*)
Oh... fancy that! (*tearfully*) You remembering it... and it so shiny... and new! (*pause, then chokingly*) Maybe I don't show it, but I am excited... about your coming back!

ROY
I... I am excited, too...

DORA
I'm so nervous my teeth are clicking...

ROY
So are mine...

DORA
And my knees are shaking like all get-out...

ROY
So are mine...

DORA
(*wailing*)
I think... I'll just sit down, and... (*sits*) try to take it all in. It's... it's like a kind of dream come true!

ROY
A dream? Will they be glad to see me?

DORA
They... they better be!

ROY

Where are they all?

DORA

Eating... Like they always do...

ROY

Let 'em have their cake! I'll (*gets bag, turns to her*) Do I still have a bed somewhere?

DORA

Back room, like always...

ROY

Don't tell 'em... yet... I'm here. I want to surprise 'em... I want... (*he takes in the room*) to just walk in... as if... there had been no twenty-nine years between it... and my walking... out... (*grins*) You think I'm an old sentimental fool, don't you? (*exit, right with bag...*)

> *Dora has risen, holding tinsel
> ... and now, standing, she touches
> it with gentle fingers, holds it to
> her cheek... and sighs from her
> very toes... as...*

Curtain for Time

WHEN CURTAIN GOES UP—*The debris is cleared up, chairs in place, gifts in a neat and inviting pile near door or fireplace or under tree...*

All signs of popcorn are gone, and tree is bright with the tinsel... the tree is as yet unlit, the lamps still lighting stage...

At first, there is no one on stage. Then, furtively, from right SALLY *enters. She is carrying a small overnight*

bag, and is dressed in coat, hat, and galoshes...
She starts, stealthily across stage, slowly and quietly to door. Left...
ROY *comes to door, right, minus his outdoor clothes and in a conspicuous checked suit. He starts into room, sees* SALLY, *pauses and watches her...*
Her hand touches door knob, she is about to open door, when—

ROY

I say...you must be Sally! SALLY *frightened, turns and he moves to her...she puts a hand to mouth stifling a scream, he goes on*: You...why, you're nearly grown, and I've never seen you! How strange...you are not like Neale ,...not even like Laura...you're more of a Corinne, aren't you?

SALLY

(*who has dropped hand and is staring at him incredulously*)
You know us...Corinne...Me? But...I...I don't remember you ... (*excited*) Are you Bill?

ROY

Bill—?

SALLY

Aunt Corinne's latest fiancé...

ROY

No. I'm only her brother...just another Martin.

SALLY

Then ... then ... you are Uncle Roy! you *must* be Uncle Roy!

ROY

(*shaking her hand*)
And **delighted** to meet you, Sally.

SALLY
(*in awe*)

Uncle Roy in the flesh—

ROY

And a new suit!—

SALLY

I never thought of you as real... somehow. You've been a family myth... for so long!

ROY

Why were you running off, Sally?

SALLY

I wasn't exactly running off. At least, I don't think I was. I was going to a party. A marvelous Christmas party in town. They... Mother and Dad, all of them... *forbade* me to go!

ROY

Oh...

SALLY

I had to go. (*pause*) You see, it's so beastly dull here.

ROY
(*laughs*)

Still that, eh—?

SALLY
(*nodding head*)

Horribly—that!

ROY
(*shaking head*)

No... only inevitably that!

SALLY

You've had adventures... all kinds of exciting times... haven't you? Seen the world? Gone everywhere? Done everything?

ROY

Well... now... yes, I guess, maybe, I did have an adventure here and there...

SALLY

Oh! (*starts for door, right*) I've got to call them . . . got to tell them you're back! *Sound of voices off, right—she turns . . . laughs . . . No need to . . . here they come!* (*He braces himself, center . . . slicks down hair, etc.,—squaring shoulders . . . and she stands a bit to side of door, right, as*)

LAURA
(*entering with* ADA)

I will say, Dora's pies are excellent . . . excellent . . . (*stops, stares at* ROY, *then* SALLY) Sally!—what are you doing in that coat? Is . . . (*turns to glare at* ROY) this your . . . (*almost gags*) Romeo? (*to Roy very rapidly*) You should be ashamed of yourself, tearing a young girl from the bosom of her family and . . . and you, old enough to be her father! You—

ADA
(*who has been transfixed, staring at* ROY, *and who now runs to him*)

It's Roy! Heaven's sakes, it's Roy!

LAURA
(*walks slowly to him*)

Roy—?

As the women cling to him and he stands grinning embarrassedly, JACK comes to door. Stuffing the last of a piece of pie into his mouth. He stops at threshold . . . Likewise staring as others have done. Then walks very hesitantly down to group wiping hands on trousers. While the excited SALLY doffs coat, hat, etc., tossing them anywhere, and then yanks off her galoshes . . . The busyness goes on right through to NEALE's entrance . . . for SALLY stops to look at ROY from time to time . . .
Meanwhile . . .

ADA
(*Holding* ROY's *arms and putting her face on it and sniffling*)
Oh, if your dear brother John were only ... alive ... to see you!

LAURA
You're older. Grown up. You've got gray hair ... I ... I (*dabs at eyes*) I could just burst out crying...

> CORINNE *and* NEALE *come in ... right. Stop as others have done.* NEALE *starts down, grinning ... then ... swiftly, he backs, thrusts hands into pockets. And stands almost belligerently ...* CORINNE *moves down gracefully and with astonished surprise ...*

CORINNE
You can't ... be Roy!

ROY
Hullo ... Corry. Where are your freckles?

CORINNE
Gone ... (*waves*) with my youth! But ... (*kisses him on cheek*) Where on earth did you find that dazzling suit? (*Looks—mock horror*) You don't own a race-track by any chance, do you?

ROY
(*grinning*)
Same old Corry!

ADA
(*spying Jack*)
Jack! Come here, and meet your dear, dead father's brother! Your own Uncle Roy—

JACK
(*awkwardly shaking hands with* ROY)
How do you do, sir?

ROY

It's like going back down the years, meeting you. John was about your age . . . when I went off . . .

NEALE

And now you've come back to gloat over us stay-at-homes, haven't you? Come back . . . to stuff . . . your . . . your . . . (*sputters*) danged glamour down our throats!

ROY

(*moving off from other and speaking quietly*)
Aren't you going . . . to say hello, Neale? Shake my hand . . . ?

NEALE

Darned if I do! (*pause, then angrily*) Where's that five dollars you borrowed from me . . . ?

ROY

Five . . . five dollars?

NEALE

Sure . . . sure . . . You've forgotten that. Just as easy as you always did forget obligations . . . and family duties . . . and everything decent!

LAURA

(*aghast*)
Why . . . Neale! Neale Martin!

CORINNE *moves to table . . . leans on it . . . facing others, and smiling . . .*

SALLY

(*discarding her last galosh with a frantic tug*)
Dad! Uncle Roy's somebody! He's been everywhere . . . had all kinds of adventures . . . !

NEALE

That's just it . . . *That's just it!* That's what makes me so all-fired mad! I . . . I . . . (*almost sobs it*) never did get anywhere . . . except to Atlantic City once, and then I got ptomaine poisoning!

LAURA
(*impressively to* ROY)
He nearly died. Such screaming as he did. I sat by his bed all night, just a-holding his hand, and—

NEALE
(*breaking in*)
We sweat and work and *stick* . . . and what do we get? It's just like Sally said . . . we only do the same darned old things over and over again . . . and him . . . (*sputtering at Roy*) he just walks off and does what he feels like doin', what he wants to do . . . and comes back and you all fall over him, like he was a *king* or somethin' . . . and you cover him all up with some kind of glory! It makes . . . me sick! Good and sick!—

ADA
Why . . . you've never said so much all at once in your whole life, Neale!

NEALE
Maybe . . . it's because you women never give me a chance. Doggone it . . . I'm nothin' but (*shakes fist at tree*) a . . . tree-trimmer! A . . . danged . . . little messenger boy . . .

ADA
(*backing*)
Oh . . . !

NEALE
And when Grandmother Martin comes down tomorrow morning . . . will she see us? Will she appreciate all the things we've done for her all these years . . . ? How we've made her comfortable, paid her little bills, taken her on outings, given up a lot of traveling and trips we might have had . . . just so's we could do more for her? Oh . . . no! She'll only . . . *see him!* And he'll strut . . . and brag . . . and prattle on . . . about *adventures* . . . *about life* . . . *about all the grand and fine things he's done* . . . and we'll be about as big and about as important as worms . . . the little, wiggley kind!

LAURA
(*who has collapsed onto sofa*)
Why ... why ... Neale! He's your brother! Roy's your own flesh and blood!

ROY
Yes ... Neale. That's why I'm home again. I am a Martin too ...

ADA
(*unexpectedly*)
If you are, Roy ... then we are not! (*to Neale*) I know how you feel ... I know exactly how you feel, because I'm getting all riled up about everything, too!

LAURA
You—?

ADA
There've been things I wanted to do ... places I wanted to see ... Corry, here, she lives in New York. They say it's a big city, and a wicked city ... but I've ... (*defiantly*) always wanted to see it ... Maybe, live in it ... !

JACK
Why—mother!

ADA
(*to him*)
Your pa—now—he was a good man. The very salt of the earth. But ... he didn't have a speck of anything exciting in his make-up. And ... anyway ... toward the last he had lumbago. And lumbago is not exactly conducive to romance.

LAURA
But, Ada! You've made a great success out of your life! You've got a fine job ... a career!

ADA
Being head-buyer for ladies' wear in a small-town department store isn't romantic! Oh, yes...laugh at me, all of you! But I'm

not so old that I don't still . . . want some of the color and life I've missed!

LAURA

You've had more'n me, Ada! Just look at me . . . a stylish stout . . . but not very stylish at that. Just plain stout. With nothing but cooking and dishwashing . . . and more dishwashing . . . to look forward to. (*raises voice*) How'd you like to be me, Ada Martin?

ADA

I wouldn't!

SALLY

Oh . . . you poor things! you *poor* things!

ROY

No! They're not to be pitied, Sally . . . I am.

SALLY

You—? (ALL *stare at him*) You've been in jail . . . like we thought . . . is that it?

ROY

No. No. (*shakes head*) I've been respectable . . . in a manner of speaking, that is. For a Martin . . . (*grins*) I've worked . . . and I've saved a bit of money.

NEALE

Money—? You've got money? (*mad all over again*) And now . . . just like in stories . . . you've come home to do all kinds of nice things for us . . . pay off the mortgage, take care of us in our old age . . . things like that! Well . . . dern ye . . . you can't do a thing for me! Not a thing. I won't let you . . . !

ROY

No . . . I'm not going to do anything for you . . . I was . . . hoping, you'd do something for me . . . !

NEALE

What? Well . . . of all the nerve! *All the blankety blank nerve!*

ROY

All I want you to do ... is forget I've been away. To let me settle down here ... smoke my pipe on the front porch, put my feet on the railing of an evening ... and at Christmas ... let me help trim the tree!

NEALE

What—? (*Others stare*)

SALLY

But ... you wouldn't want to do that! It'd be awful, Uncle Roy! Simply awful!

ROY

I never served time in jail. I'm not exactly what you'd call a bum. But, I'm not a glittering ... howling success either ... (*touches suit*) When I bought this, I meant to *look* the part. To look like I was somebody that amounted to something. I wanted to show off ... to strut ... just like Neale said I did ... I'd have let you think I had had a fine time out of life. I wanted to ... have you think that ... but ... (*waves hands, and grins sheepishly*) I've not done anything that was a whit more exciting or bigger than anything you've done ... things got pretty dull for me, too!

LAURA

What ... what have you done, Roy?

ROY

I ... well ... fact is, I've been on the railroad. A brakeman on the P. and E.

NEALE

The P. and E.? But ... that ... that line runs right through and past this town!

ROY

Sure. And everytime I whizzed by, I'd look out ... and try to see the house ... never could though ...

NEALE
Well . . . I'll be . . . (*pause, then louder*) I'll be!—(to ROY) You mean . . . you've never been anywhere?

ROY
To the end of the line and back . . . *Year* after Year. . . .

CORINNE
(*laughing*)
That's all we do, isn't it, we Martins? Go to the end of the line and back—?

ADA
Not you, Corry!

SALLY
You . . . you've got everything!

CORINNE
No. Sally. I . . . I have nothing! (*voice rises*) Nothing at all . . . (*pause—then rapidly*) Bill is in New York. We had a quarrel and he is . . . alone . . . or maybe . . . not alone . . . ! But, just as you guessed, he isn't in South America!

LAURA
Oh . . . Corry! (*wails it*) You spoiled his Christmas!

DORA *comes to door, right— starts to talk—stops—and waits: as . . .*

CORINNE
I've made fun of you . . . teased you . . . acted superior! Pretended to despise your knitting . . . your little homey gossip . . . your everyday kind of living! But I . . . didn't. Or . . . why did I come back for a bit of it . . . Christmas after Christmas? Things . . .

(*waves*) out there ... aren't any better. Nothing ... in all the world is any better ... than just being a Martin!

ROY
(*fervently*)
Ditto!

DORA
Miss Corinne ... your call came through ...(*bluntly*) New York!

CORINNE
Oh! (*runs to door*) right ... exit.

The others look at each other a bit uneasily ... ROY *stands—hands clasped at back, staring up at tree:*
SALLY *hurls a cushion at* JACK, *who ducks ... and it hits* DORA ... *who, matter of factly, catches it, and fluffs it out, then puts it back to its place ... crossing phlegmatically ... as ...*

SALLY
Hi ... *Dear* cousin!

JACK
(*grinning*)
Hi ...

Off stage—comes CORINNE'S *voice—*
Immediately, all stiffen, and without any pretense, proceed to listen ... with avid interest ...

CORINNE
Oh, hello, Bill ... no! there's not been an accident. Wanted to say, Merry Christmas, that's all ... (*pause*) Oh ... (*voice catches*)

so am I . . . oh, Bill, . . . so am I lonely . . . terribly sorry and so terribly lonely! (*pause*) Will you—? Oh, Bill . . . Billy . . . *Darling!*

> —Silence . . .
> And then, CORINNE, *appears, right* . . . *half crying, half laughing* . . .

That was Bill! He's . . . coming here, by plane . . . he'll be here . . . Tomorrow. (*comes on down*) He was lonely. Can you imagine that? All of New York to spend Christmas in . . . and he was . . . (*catch again in voice*) Lonely! (*pause*) I guess . . . maybe, Bill's just average family, too! (*to* NEALE) He's a lot . . . like you are, Neale. That's . . . That's why I love him . . . why . . . I'm going to marry him before we return to New York! (*covers eyes with hands*) Oh . . . I'm so happy . . . so *terribly happy!*

> *All are blinking eyes. Etc. . . . as* . . .

DORA
(*bluntly, arms a-kimbo*)
That there tinsel looks real nice and bright on the tree, don't it?

SALLY
Oh . . . yes! Oh, yes, indeed! It's the . . . nicest and brightest tinsel . . . in . . . (*rising voice*) all the world!
> *Bells ring out* . . .

JACK
It's Christmas . . . !

CORINNE
(*raising head and listening*)
Christmas!

DORA

(*who has gone to door, right*)
She's coming down! Grandmother Martin's coming . . . I can hear her!

The bells fade so that voices can be heard above them . . . but they continue to ring, off . . . as . . .

ADA

Neale! Quick . . . turn on the tree lights!

All except LAURA, ROY *and* DORA *rush around turning off lamps as* NEALE *turns on tree lights . . . So that the stage is lit with them, and a soft, reflected light from beyond the door, right, where presumably there's a hall.*

LAURA

(*grabbing* ROY *and pushing him to center, left*)
There . . . you stand like that . . . so she'll see you . . . right off! Oh . . . what a Christmas this is turning out to be! I . . . I could . . . just bust out crying!

ROY *is satisfactorily arranged, and others are in a little welcoming group, this time, ready to welcome Grandmother Martin as she will step from door right, to room . . . all face in that direction . . .*

JACK

What'll it be? Silent Night?

ADA

Hurry . . . start the tune, somebody!

CORINNE

Let's make it ... "O, little town ...

> (*Her voice goes into the carol*) *of Bethlehem, how still we see thee lie ..."*
>
> DORA *holds back the drape at door, right and joins her ... then, the others pick it up ... and they are singing it ... with the bells ringing softly off stage as ...*

(*Curtain*)

If this little play is given as part of a Christmas entertainment, in church or club: The following is suggested, in order to make the audience part of the entertainment itself:

The gifts of the stage, can be, in reality, the gifts to be distributed to the children or others ...

And as the curtain falls, the singing on stage is fainter ... as Roy or another character appears before curtain announcing ...

> "Don't go ... join in with us!
> Let's make the rafters ring!
> Come on ... Everybody!"

And up goes the curtain again, with those on the stage, now facing audience ... and singing lustily, the audience to join in. Other carols might follow ...

With NEALE *or another character donning Santa Claus whiskers and hat at the finale, and inviting those who are to receive gifts up to the stage to get them.*

CHAPTER VII

CHRISTMAS POETRY AND STORIES

CHRISTMAS STORIES and poems bring pleasant memories in the minds of those to whom the Day means so much. When the children and grandchildren come home to be with Father and Mother again, that nice old custom of interspersing recitations with carol singing is one that should be continued or renewed if it has been dropped in the flow of the years under the bridge of Time.

To a selection of old favorites which are as much a part of Christmas as the tree itself, we have added others of more modern origin. They have been chosen to appeal to all members of the family, young and old. They may also be used as recitations at the church or school Christmas entertainment, and in some cases, a talented individual in a group can be prevailed upon to give a reading at a party or home circle.

The poems and stories serve other purposes. To the man or woman who is away from home, either to school or college, the practice of reading aloud is one to be encouraged. It is a sure-fire antidote for loneliness and at the same time, helps a lot to acquire a well modulated voice. The next time you feel depressed or bored, turn to the stories and poems in this Christmas companion, and read them aloud, slowly and distinctly, giving each word its proper accent and tone. You will be pleased with the result!

CHRISTMAS: A DEFINITION *
By Clement A. Miles

Christmas is a microcosm of world religion. It reflects almost every phase of thought and feeling from crude magic and superstition to the speculative mysticism of Eckhart, from the mere delight in physical indulgence to the exquisite spirituality of St. Francis.

Ascetic and bon-vivant, mystic and materialist, learned and simple, noble and peasant, all have found something in it on which to lay hold. It is a river into which have flowed tributaries from every side, from Oriental religion, from Greek and Roman civilization, from Celtic, Teutonic, Slav and probably pre-Aryan society, all mingling their waters so that it is often hard to discover the far-away springs.

At no time has so much been made of children as today, and because Christmas is their feast its luster continues unabated in an age upon which dogmatic Christianity has largely lost its hold, which laughs at the pagan superstitions of its forefathers.

Christmas is the feast of the beginnings, of instinctive happy childhood; the Christian idea of the Immortal Babe renewing weary, stained humanity. It blends with the thought of the New Year, with its hope and promise, laid in the cradle of Time.

* (From *Christmas in Ritual and Tradition*, published 1912 in England by T. Fisher Unwin.)

IS THERE A SANTA CLAUS?
By Francis P. Church

FORTY-THREE years ago, September 21, 1897, there appeared an editorial in *The New York Sun* which has since become a classic of American Christmas-lore. It was headed "Is There a Santa Claus?" and was written by Francis Pharcellus Church, who was born in Rochester, New York, on February 22, 1839, and died in New York on April 11, 1906. The origin of the Santa Claus article is best described by Edward P. Mitchell, who was in charge of *The Sun's* editorial page when the article was written. Mr. Mitchell says in his *Memoirs of an Editor:*

"For thirty-five years and until his death in 1906 Frank Church was a regular contributor to *The Sun's* editorial page. His lifetime lasted for four years beyond the date when I became editor-in-chief and for that period he was my alternate. There was never a more delightful associate. Quick of perception of the interesting in every phase of human activity except politics (for which he cared little, bless his soul!), there was in his features something of that gentlemanly pugnacity seen in the faces of the type of Richard Olney's and Thomas Nelson Page's— a latent aggressiveness that marred neither the delicacy of his fancy nor the warmth of his sympathies.

"One day in 1897 I handed to him a letter that had come in the mail from a child of eight, saying: 'Please tell me the truth, is there a Santa Claus?' Her little friends had told her No. Church bristled and poohpoohed at the subject when I suggested that he write a reply to Virginia O'Hanlon; but he took the letter and turned with an air of resignation to his desk. In a short time he had produced the article which has probably been reprinted during the past quarter of a century, as a classic expression of Christmas sentiment, more millions of times than any other newspaper article ever written by any newspaper writer in any language. Even yet no holiday season approaches without bringing to the newspaper requests from all over the land for the exact text for repeated use on Christmas Day."

Here is the complete and original copy:

Is THERE A SANTA CLAUS?

We take pleasure in answering at once and thus prominently the communication below, expressing at the same time our great gratification that its faithful author is numbered among the friends of *The Sun*:

> "Dear Editor—I am 8 years old.
> "Some of my little friends say there is no Santa Claus.
> "Papa says 'If you see it in *The Sun* it's so.'
> "Please tell me the truth, is there a Santa Claus?
> <div align="right">"<i>Virginia O'Hanlon.</i></div>
> "115 West Ninety-fifth street."

Virginia, your little friends are wrong. They have been affected by the skepticism of a skeptical age. They do not believe except they see. They think that nothing can be which is not comprehensible by their little minds. All minds, Virginia, whether they be men's or children's, are little. In this great universe of ours man is a mere insect, an ant, in his intellect, as compared with the boundless world about him, as measured by the intelligence capable of grasping the whole of truth and knowledge.

Yes, Virginia, there is a Santa Claus. He exists as certainly as love and generosity and devotion exist, and you know that they abound and give to your life its highest beauty and joy. Alas! how dreary would be the world if there were no Santa Claus! It would be as dreary as if there were no Virginias. There would be no childlike faith then, no poetry, no romance to make tolerable this existence. We should have no enjoyment, except in sense and sight. The eternal light with which childhood fills the world would be extinguished.

Not believe in Santa Claus! You might as well not believe in fairies! You might get your papa to hire men to watch in all the chimneys on Christmas Eve to catch Santa Claus, but even if they did not see Santa Claus coming down, what would that prove? Nobody sees Santa Claus, but that is no sign that there is no Santa Claus. The most real things in the world are those that neither children nor men can see. Did you ever see fairies dancing on the lawn? Of course not, but that's no proof that they are not there. Nobody can conceive or imagine all the wonders there are unseen and unseeable in the world.

You tear apart the baby's rattle and see what makes the noise inside, but there is a veil covering the unseen world which not the strongest man, nor even the united strength of all the strongest men that ever lived, could tear apart. Only faith, fancy, poetry, love, romance, can push aside that curtain and view and picture the supernal beauty and glory beyond. Is it all real? Ah, Virginia, in all this world there is nothing else real and abiding.

No Santa Claus! Thank God! he lives, and he lives forever. A thousand years from now, Virginia, nay, ten times ten thousand years from now, he will continue to make glad the heart of childhood.

AT BRACEBRIDGE HALL

By Washington Irving

THE dinner was served up in the great hall, where the Squire always held his Christmas banquet. A blazing crackling fire of logs had been heaped on to warm the spacious apartment, and the flame went sparkling and wreathing up the wide-mouthed chimney. The great picture of the crusader and his white horse had been profusely decorated with greens for the occasion; and the holly and ivy had likewise been wreathed round the helmet and the weapons on the opposite wall, which I understood were the arms of the same warrior. I must own, by the bye, I had strong doubts about the authenticity of the painting and armour as having belonged to the crusader, they certainly having the stamp of more recent days; but I as told that the painting had been so considered time out of mind; and that as to the armour, it had been found in a lumber room, and elevated to its present situation by the Squire, who at once determined it to be the armour of the family hero; and as he was absolute authority on all such subjects in his own household, the matter had passed into current acceptation. A sideboard was set out just under this chivalric trophy, on which was a display of plate that might have vied (at least in variety) with Belshazzar's parade of the vessels of the temple; "flagons, cans, cups, beakers, goblets, basins, and embers"; the gorgeous utensils of good companionship, that had gradually accumulated through many generations of jovial housekeepers. Before these stood two Yule candles beaming like two stars of the first magnitude; other lights were distributed in branches, and the whole array glittered like a firmament of silver.

CHRISTMAS POETRY AND STORIES 161

We were ushered into this banqueting scene with the sound of minstrelsy, the old harper being seated on a stool beside the fireplace, and twanging his instrument with a vast deal more power than melody. Never did Christmas board display a more goodly and gracious assemblage of countenances: those who were not handsome were, at least, happy; and happiness is a rare improver of your hard-favoured visage. I always consider an old English family as well worth studying as a collection of Holbein's portraits or Albert Durer's prints. There is much antiquarian lore to be acquired; much knowledge of the physiognomies of former times. Perhaps it may be from having continually before their eyes those rows of old family portraits, with which the mansions of this country are stocked: certain it is, that the quaint features of antiquity are often most faithfully perpetuated in these ancient lines; and I have traced an old family nose through a whole picture gallery, legitimately handed down from generation to generation, almost from the time of the Conquest. Something of the kind was to be observed in the worthy company around me. Many of their faces had evidently originated in a Gothic age, and been merely copied by succeeding generations; and there was one little girl, in particular, of staid demeanour, with a high Roman nose, and an antique vinegar aspect, who was a great favourite of the Squire's, being, as he said, a Bracebridge all over, and the very counterpart of one of his ancestors who figured in the court of Henry VIII.

The parson said grace, which was not a short familiar one, such as is commonly addressed to the Deity, in these unceremonious days; but a long, courtly, well-worded one of the ancient school. There was now a pause, as if something was expected; when suddenly the butler entered the hall with some degree of bustle; he was attended by a servant on each side with a large wax-light, and bore a silver dish, on which was an enormous pig's head decorated with rosemary, with a lemon in its mouth, which was placed with great formality at the head of the table. The moment this pageant made its appearance, the harper struck up a flourish; at the conclusion of which the young Oxonian, on receiving a hint from the Squire, gave, with an air of the most comic gravity, an old carol, the first verse of which was as follows:

Caput apri defero
Reddens laudes Domino.
The boar's head in hand bring I,
With garlands gay and rosemary.
I pray you all sing merrily
Qui estis in convivio.

Though prepared to witness many of these little eccentricities, from being apprised of the peculiar hobby of mine host; yet, I confess, the parade with which so odd a dish was introduced somewhat perplexed me, until I gathered from the conversation of the Squire and the parson that it was meant to represent the bringing in of the boar's head: a dish formerly served up with much ceremony, and the sound of minstrelsy and song, at great tables on Christmas day. "I like the old custom," said the Squire, "not merely because it is stately and pleasing in itself, but because it was observed at the College of Oxford, at which I was educated. When I hear the old song chanted, it brings to mind the time when I was young and gamesome—and the noble old college-hall—and my fellow students loitering about in their black gowns; many of whom, poor lads, are now in their graves!"

The parson, however, whose mind was not haunted by such associations, and who was always more taken up with the text than the sentiment, objected to the Oxonian's version of the carol: which he affirmed was different from that sung at college. He went on, with the dry perseverance of a commentator, to give the college reading, accompanied by sundry annotations: addressing himself at first to the company at large; but finding their attention gradually diverted to other talk, and other objects, he lowered his tone as his number of auditors diminished, until he concluded his remarks, in an under voice, to a fat-headed old gentleman next him, who was silently engaged in the discussion of a huge plateful of turkey.

The table was literally loaded with good cheer, and presented an epitome of country abundance, in this season of overflowing larders. A distinguished post was allotted to "ancient sirloin," as mine host termed it; being, as he added, "the standard of old English hospitality, and a joint of goodly presence, and full of expectation." There were several dishes quaintly decorated, and which had evidently something traditionary in their embellishments; but about which, as I did not like to appear over-curious, I asked no questions.

I could not, however, but notice a pie, magnificently decorated with peacocks' feathers, in imitation of the tail of that bird, which overshadowed a considerable tract of the table. This the Squire confessed, with some little hesitation, was a pheasant-pie, though a peacock-pie was certainly the most authentical; but there had been such a mortality among the peacocks this season, that he could not prevail upon himself to have one killed.

When the cloth was removed, the butler brought in a huge silver vessel of rare and curious workmanship, which he placed before the Squire. Its appearance was hailed with acclamation; being the Wassail Bowl, so renowned in Christmas festivity. The contents had been prepared by the Squire himself; for it was a beverage in the skilful mixture of which he particularly prided himself; alleging that it was too abstruse and complex for the comprehension of an ordinary servant. It was a potation, indeed, that might well make the heart of a toper leap within him; being composed of the richest and raciest wines, highly spiced and sweetened, with roasted apples bobbing about the surface.

The old gentleman's whole countenance beamed with a serene look of indwelling delight, as he stirred this mighty bowl. Having raised it to his lips, with a hearty wish of a merry Christmas to all present, he sent it brimming round the board, for every one to follow his example, according to the primitive style; pronouncing it "the ancient fountain of good feeling, where all hearts met together."

There was much laughing and rallying as the honest emblem of Christmas joviality circulated, and was kissed rather coyly by the ladies. When it reached Master Simon he raised it in both hands, and with the air of a boon companion struck up an old Wassail chanson....

Much of the conversation during dinner turned upon family topics, to which I was a stranger. There was, however, a great deal of rallying of Master Simon about some gay widow, with whom he was accused of having a flirtation. This attack was commenced by the ladies; but it was continued throughout the dinner by the fat-headed old gentleman next the parson, with the persevering assiduity of a slow-hound; being one of those long-winded jokers, who, though rather dull at starting game, are unrivalled for their talents in hunting it down. At every pause in the general conversation, he renewed his bantering in pretty much the same terms; winking hard at me with both eyes whenever he gave Master Simon what he considered a home thrust. The latter, indeed, seemed fond of being teased on the subject, as old bachelors are apt to be; and he took occasion to inform me, in an undertone, that the lady in question was a prodigiously fine woman, and drove her own curricle.

The dinner-time passed away in this flow of innocent hilarity; and, though the old hall may have resounded in its time with many a scene of broader rout and revel, yet I doubt whether it ever witnessed more honest and genuine enjoyment. How easy it is for one benevolent being to diffuse pleasure around him; and how truly is a kind heart a fountain of gladness, making everything in its vicinity to freshen into smiles! The joyous disposition of the worthy Squire was perfectly contagious; he was happy himself, and disposed to make all the world happy; and the little eccentricities of his humor did but season, in a manner, the sweetness of his philanthropy.

When the ladies had retired, the conversation, as usual, became still more animated; many good things were broached which had been thought of during dinner, but which would not exactly do for a lady's ear; and though I cannot positively affirm that there was much wit uttered, yet I have certainly heard many contests of rare wit produce much less laughter. I found the tide of wine and wassail fast gaining on the dry land of sober judgment. The company grew merrier and louder as their jokes grew duller. Master Simon was in as chirping a humour as a grasshopper filled with dew; his old songs grew of a warmer complexion, and he began to talk maudlin about the widow. He even gave a long song about the wooing of a widow, which he informed me he had gathered from an excellent black-letter work, entitled "Cupid's Solicitor for Love, containing store of good advice for bachelors," and which he promised to lend me. The first verse was to this effect:

He that will woo a widow must not dally,
   He must make hay while the sun doth shine;
He must not stand with her, Shall I, Shall I?
   But boldly say, Widow, thou must be mine.

This song inspired the fat-headed old gentleman, who made several attempts to tell a rather broad story out of Joe Miller, that was pat to the purpose; but he always stuck in the middle, everybody recollecting the latter part excepting himself. The parson, too, began to show the effects of good cheer, having gradually settled down into a doze, and his wig sitting most suspiciously on one side. Just at this juncture we were summoned to the drawing-room, and, I suspect, at the private instigation of mine host, whose joviality seemed always tempered with a proper love of decorum.

After the dinner-table was removed, the hall was given up to the younger members of the family, who, prompted to all kind of noisy mirth by the Oxonian and Master Simon, made its old walls ring with their merriment, as they played at romping games. I delight in witnessing the gambols of children, and particularly at this happy holiday-season, and could not help stealing out of the drawing room on hearing one of their peals of laughter. I found them at the game of blind-man's buff. Master Simon, who was the leader of their revels, and seemed on all occasions to fulfil the office of that ancient potentate, the Lord of Misrule, was blinded in the midst of the hall. The little beings were as busy about him as the mock fairies about Falstaff, pinching him, plucking at the skirts of his coat, and tickling him with straws. One fine blue-eyed girl of about thirteen, with her flaxen hair all in beautiful confusion, her frolic face in a glow, her frock half torn off her shoulders, a complete picture of a romp, was the chief tormentor; and from the slyness with which Master Simon avoided the smaller game, and hemmed this wild little nymph in corners, and obliged her to jump shrieking over chairs, I suspected the rogue of being not a whit more blinded than was convenient....

Whilst we were all attention to the parson's stories, our ears were suddenly assailed by a burst of heterogeneous sounds from the hall, in which was mingled something like the clang of rude minstrelsy, with the uproar of many small voices and girlish laughter. The door suddenly flew open, and a train came trooping into the room, that might almost have been mistaken for the breaking up of the court of Fairy. That indefatigable spirit, Master Simon, in the faithful discharge of his duties as Lord of Misrule, had conceived the idea of a Christmas mummery, or masking; and having called in to his assistance the Oxonian and the young officer, who were equally ripe for anything that should occasion romping and merriment, they had carried it into instant effect. The old housekeeper had been consulted; the antique clothes-presses and wardrobes rummaged and made to yield up the relics of finery that had not seen the light for several generations; the younger part of the company had been privately convened from the parlour and hall, and the whole had been bedizened out, into a burlesque imitation of an antique masque.

Master Simon led the van, as "Ancient Christmas," quaintly apparelled in a ruff, a short cloak, which had very much the aspect of one of the old housekeeper's petticoats, and a hat that might have served for a village steeple, and must indubitably have figured in the days of the Covenanters. From under this his nose curved boldly forth, flushed with a frost-bitten bloom, that seemed the very trophy of a December blast. He was accompanied by the blue-eyed romp, dished up as "Dame Mince-Pie," in the venerable magnificence of faded brocade, long stomacher, peaked hat, and high-heeled shoes. The young officer appeared as Robin Hood, in a sporting dress of Kendal green, and a foraging cap with a gold tassel. The costume, to be sure, did not bear testimony to deep research and there was an evident eye to the picturesque, natural to a young gallant in the presence of his mistress. The fair Julia hung on his arm in a pretty rustic dress, as "Maid Marian."

The rest of the train had been metamorphosed in various ways; the girls trussed up in the finery of the ancient belles of the Bracebridge line, and the striplings bewhiskered with burnt cork, and gravely clad in broad skirts, hanging sleeves, and full-bottomed wigs, to represent the characters of Roast Beef, Plum Pudding, and other worthies celebrated in ancient maskings. The whole was under the control of the Oxonian, in the appropriate character of Misrule; and I observed that he exercised rather a mischievous sway with his wand over the smaller personages of the pageant.

The irruption of this motley crew, with beat of drum, according to ancient custom, was the consummation of uproar and merriment. Master Simon covered himself with glory by the stateliness with which, as Ancient Christmas, he walked a minuet with the peerless, though giggling, Dame Mince-Pie. It was followed by a dance of all the characters, which, from its medley of costumes, seemed as though the old family portraits had skipped down from their frames to join in the sport. Different centuries were figuring at cross hands and right and left; the dark ages were cutting pirouettes and rigadoons; and the days of Queen Bess jigging merrily down the middle, through a line of succeeding generations.

The worthy Squire contemplated these fantastic sports, and this resurrection of his old wardrobe, with the simple relish of childish delight. He stood chuckling and rubbing his hands, and scarcely hearing a word the parson said, notwithstanding that the latter was discoursing most authentically on the ancient and stately dance of Paon, or Peacock, from which he conceived the minuet to be derived. For my part, I was in a continual excitement, from the varied scenes of whim and innocent gaiety passing before me. It was inspiring to see wild-eyed frolic and warm-hearted hospitality breaking out from among the chills and glooms of winter, and old age throwing off his apathy, and catching once more the freshness of youthful enjoyment. I felt also an interest in the scene, from the consideration that these fleeting customs were posting fast into oblivion, and that this was, perhaps, the only family in England in which the whole of them were still punctiliously observed. There was a quaintness, too, mingled with all this revelry that gave it a peculiar zest; it was suited to the time and place; and as the old Manor House almost reeled with mirth and wassail, it seemed echoing back the joviality of long-departed years.

THE FIR TREE

By Hans Christian Andersen

OUT in the woods stood a nice little Fir tree. The place he had was a very good one; the sun shone on him; as to fresh air, there was enough of that, and round him grew many large-sized comrades, pines as well as firs. But the little Fir wanted so very much to be a grown-up tree.

He did not think of the warm sun and of the fresh air; he did not care for the little cottage children that ran about and prattled when they were in the woods looking for wild strawberries. The children often came with a whole pitcher full of berries, or a long row of them threaded on a straw, and sat down near the young tree and said, "Oh, how pretty he is! what a nice little fir!" But this was what the Tree could not bear to hear.

At the end of a year he had shot up a good deal, and after another year he was another long bit taller; for with fir trees one can always tell by the shoots how many years old they are.

"Oh, were I but such a high tree as the others are!" sighed he. "Then I should be able to spread out my branches, and with the tops to look into the wide world! Then would the birds build nests among my branches; and when there was a breeze, I could bend with as much stateliness as the others!"

Neither the sunbeams, nor the birds, nor the red clouds, which morning and evening sailed above them, gave the little Tree any pleasure.

In winter, when the snow lay glittering on the ground, a hare would often come leaping along, and jump right over the little Tree. Oh, that made him so angry! But two winters were past, and in the third the Tree was so large that the hare was obliged to go around it. "To grow and grow, to get older and be tall," thought the Tree—"that, after all, is the most delightful thing in the world!"

In autumn the woodcutters always came and felled some of the largest trees. This happened every year; and the young Fir tree, that had now grown to a very comely size, trembled at the sight; for the magnificent great trees fell to the earth with noise and cracking, the branches were lopped off, and the trees looked long and bare; they were hardly to be recognized; and then they were laid in carts, and the horses dragged them out of the woods.

Where did they go to? What became of them?

In spring, when the Swallows and the Storks came, the Tree asked them, "Don't you know where they have been taken? Have you not met them anywhere?"

The Swallows did not know anything about it; but the Stork looked musing, nodded his head, and said: "Yes, I think I know; I met many ships as I was flying hither from Egypt; on the ships were magnificent masts, and I venture to assert that it was they that smelt so of fir. I may congratulate you, for they lifted themselves on high most majestically!"

"Oh, were I but old enough to fly across the sea! But how does the sea look in reality? What is it like?"

"That would take a long time to explain," said the Stork, and with these words off he went.

"Rejoice in thy growth!" said the Sunbeams, "rejoice in thy vigorous growth, and in the fresh life that moveth within thee!"

And the Wind kissed the Tree, and the Dew wept tears over him; but the Fir understood it not.

When Christmas came, quite young trees were cut down; trees which often were not even as large or of the same age as this Fir tree, who could never rest, but always wanted to be off. These young trees, and they were always the finest looking, retained their branches; they were laid on carts, and the horses drew them out of the woods.

"Where are they going to?" asked the Fir. "They are not taller than I; there was one indeed that was considerably shorter and why do they retain all their branches? Whither are they taken?"

"We know! we know!" chirped the Sparrows. "We have peeped

in at the windows in the town below! We know whither they are taken! The greatest splendor and the greatest magnificence one can imagine await them. We peeped through the windows, and saw them planted in the middle of the warm room, and ornamented with the most splendid things—with gilded apples, with gingerbread, with toys, and many hundred lights!"

"And then?" asked the Fir tree, trembling in every bough. "And then? What happens then?"

"We did not see anything more: it was incomparably beautiful."

"I would fain know if I am destined for so glorious a career," cried the Tree, rejoicing. "That is still better than to cross the sea! What a longing do I suffer! Were Christmas but come! I am now tall, and my branches spread like the others that were carried off last year! Oh, were I but already on the cart! Were I in the warm room with all the splendor and magnificence! Yes; then something better, something still grander, will surely follow, or wherefore should they thus ornament me? Something better, grander, must follow—but what? Oh, how long, how I suffer! I do not know myself what is the matter with me!"

"Rejoice in our presence!" said the Air and the Sunlight; "rejoice in thy own fresh youth!"

But the Tree did not rejoice at all; he grew and grew, and was green both winter and summer. People that saw him said, "What a fine tree!" and toward Christmas he was one of the first that was cut down. The axe struck deep into the very pith; the Tree fell to the earth with a sigh; he felt a pang—it was like a swoon; he could not think of happiness, for he was sorrowful at being separated from his home, from the place where he had sprung up. He knew well that he should never see his dear old comrades, the little bushes and flowers around him, any more; perhaps not even the birds! The departure was not at all agreeable.

The Tree came to himself when he was unloaded in a courtyard with the other trees, and heard a man say, "That one is splendid! we don't want the others." Then two servants came in rich livery and carried the Fir tree into a large and splendid drawing-room. Portraits were hanging on the walls, and near the white porcelain stove stood two large Chinese vases with lions on the covers. There, too, were large easy chairs, silken sofas, large tables full of picture-books, and full of toys worth hundreds and hundreds of crowns—

at least the children said so. And the Fir tree was stuck upright in a cask that was filled with sand; but no one could see that it was a cask, for green cloth was hung all around it, and it stood on a large gayly colored carpet. Oh, how the Tree quivered! What was to happen? The servants, as well as the young ladies, decorated it. On one branch there hung little nets cut out of colored paper, and each net was filled with sugar-plums; and among the other boughs gilded apples and walnuts were suspended, looking as though they had grown there, and little blue and white tapers were placed among the leaves. Dolls that looked for all the world like men—the Tree had never beheld such before—were seen among the foliage, and at the very top a large star of gold tinsel was fixed. It was really splendid—beyond description splendid.

"This evening!" said they all; "how it will shine this evening!"

"Oh," thought the Tree, "if the evening were but come! If the tapers were but lighted! And then I wonder what will happen! Perhaps the other trees from the forest will come to look at me! Perhaps the Sparrows will beat against the window-panes! I wonder if I shall take root here, and winter and summer stand covered with ornaments!"

He knew very much about the matter! but he was so impatient that for sheer longing he got a pain in his back, and this with trees is the same thing as a headache with us.

The candles were now lighted. What brightness! What splendor! The Tree trembled so in every bough that one of the tapers set fire to the foliage. It blazed up splendidly.

"Help! Help!" cried the young ladies, and they quickly put out the fire.

Now the Tree did not even dare tremble. What a state he was in. He was so uneasy lest he should lose something of his splendor, that he was quite bewildered amidst the glare and brightness; when suddenly both folding-doors opened, and a troop of children rushed in as if they would upset the Tree. The older persons followed quietly; the little ones stood quite still. But it was only for a moment; then they shouted so that the whole place reechoed with their rejoicing; they danced around the Tree, and one present after the other was pulled off.

"What are they about?'" thought the Tree. "What is to happen now?" And the lights burned down to the very branches, and as they burned down they were put out, one after the other, and then the children had permission to plunder the Tree. So they fell upon it with such violence that all its branches cracked; if it had not been fixed firmly in the cask, it would certainly have tumbled down.

The children danced about with their beautiful playthings: no one looked at the Tree except the old nurse, who peeped between the branches but it was only to see if there was a fig or an apple left that had been forgotten.

"A story! a story!" cried the children, drawing a little fat man toward the Tree. He seated himself under it, and said: "Now we are in the shade, and the Tree can listen, too. But I shall tell only one story. Now which will you have: that about Ivedy-Avedy, or about Klumpy-Dumpy who tumbled downstairs, and yet after all came to the throne and married the princess?"

"Ivedy-Avedy!" cried some; "Klumpy-Dumpy!" cried the others. There was such a bawling and screaming—the Fir tree alone was silent, and he thought to himself, "Am I not to bawl with the rest?—am I to do nothing whatever?" for he was one of the company and had done what he had to do.

And the man told about Klumpy-Dumpy that tumbled down, who notwithstanding came to the throne, and at last married the princess. And the children clapped their hands and cried out, "Oh, go on! Do go on!" They wanted to hear about Ivedy-Avedy, too, but the little man only told them about Klumpy-Dumpy. The Fir tree stood quite still and absorbed in thought; the birds in the woods had never related the like of this. "Klumpy-Dumpy fell downstairs, and yet he married the princess! Yes! Yes! That's the way of the world!" thought the Fir tree, and believed it all, because the man who told the story was so good-looking. "Well, well! who knows, perhaps I may fall downstairs, too, and get a princess as a wife!" And he looked forward with joy to the morrow, when he hoped to be decked out again with lights, playthings, fruits, and tinsel.

"I won't tremble tomorrow," thought the Fir tree. "I will enjoy to the full all my splendor. Tomorrow I shall hear again the story of Klumpy-Dumpy, and perhaps that of Ivedy-Avedy, too." And the whole night the Tree stood still and in deep thought.

In the morning the servant and the housemaid came in.

"Now, then, the splendor will begin again," thought the Fir. But they dragged him out of the room, and up the stairs into the loft; and here in a dark corner, here no daylight could enter, they left him. "What's the meaning of this?" thought the Tree. "What am I to do here? What shall I hear now, I wonder?" And he leaned against the wall, lost in reverie. Time enough had he, too, for his reflections; for days and nights passed on, and nobody came up; and when at last somebody did come, it as only to put some great trunks in a corner out of the way. There stood the Tree quite hidden; it seemed as if he had been entirely forgotten.

"'Tis now winter out of doors!" thought the Tree. "The earth is hard and covered with snow; men cannot plant me now, and therefore I have been put up here under shelter till the springtime comes! How thoughtful that is! How kind man is, after all! If it only were not so dark here, and so terribly lonely! Not even a hare. And out in the woods it was so pleasant, when the snow was on the ground, and the hare leaped by; yes—even when he jumped over me; but I did not like it then. It is really terribly lonely here!"

"Squeak! squeak!" said a little Mouse at the same moment, peeping out of his hole. And then another little one came. They sniffed about the Fir tree, and rustled among the branches.

"It is dreadfully cold," said the Mouse. "But for that, it would be delightful here, old Fir, wouldn't it?"

"I am by no means old," said the Fir tree. "There's many a one considerably older than I am."

"Where do you come from," asked the Mice; "and what can you do?" They were so extremely curious. "Tell us about the most beautiful spot on the earth. Have you never been there? Were you never in the larder, where cheeses lie on the shelves, and hams hang from above; where one dances about on tallow-candles; that place where one enters lean, and comes out again fat and portly?"

"I know no such place," said the Tree, "but I know the woods, where the sun shines, and where the little birds sing." And then he told them all about his youth; and the little Mice had never heard the like before; and they listened and said:

"Well, to be sure! How much you have seen! How happy you must have been!"

"I?" said the Fir tree, thinking over what he had himself related.

"Yes, in reality those were happy times." And then he told about Christmas Eve, when he was decked out with cakes and candles.

"Oh," said the little Mice, "how fortunate you have been, old Fir tree!"

"I am by no means old," said he. "I came from the woods this winter; I am in my prime, and am only rather short for my age."

"What delightful stories you know!" said the Mice; and the next night they came with four other little Mice, who were to hear what the tree recounted; and the more he related, the more plainly he remembered all himself; and it appeared as if those times had really been happy times. "But they may still come—they may still come. Klumpy-Dumpy fell downstairs and yet he got a princess," and he thought at the moment of a nice little Birch tree growing out in the woods, to the Fir, that would be a real charming princess.

"Who is Klumpy-Dumpy?" asked the Mice. So then the Fir tree told the whole fairy tale, for he could remember every single word of it; and the little Mice jumped for joy up to the very top of the Tree. Next night two more Mice came, and on Sunday two Rats, even; but they said the stories were not interesting, which vexed the little Mice; and they, too, now began to think them not so very amusing either.

"Do you know only one story?" asked the Rats.

"Only that one," answered the Tree. "I heard it on my happiest evening; but I did not then know how happy I was."

"It is a very stupid story. Don't you know one about bacon and tallow candles? Can't you tell any larder stories?"

"No," said the Tree.

"Then good-bye," said the Rats; and they went home.

At last the little Mice stayed away also; and the Tree sighed: "After all, it was very pleasant when the sleek little Mice sat around me and listened to what I told them. Now that too is over. But I will take good care to enjoy myself when I am brought out again."

But when was that to be? Why, one morning there came a quantity of people and set to work in the loft. The trunks were moved, the Tree was pulled out and thrown—rather hard, it is true—down on the floor, but a man drew him toward the stairs, where the daylight shone.

"Now a merry life will begin again," thought the Tree. He felt the fresh air, the first sunbeam—and now he was out in the courtyard. All passed so quickly, there was so much going on around him, that the Tree quite forgot to look to himself. The court adjoined a garden, and all was in flower; the roses hung so fresh and odorous over the balustrade, the lindens were in blossom, the Swallows flew by, and said, "Quirre-vit! my husband is come!" but it was not the Fir tree that they meant.

"Now, then, I shall really enjoy life," said he, exultingly, and spread out his branches; but alas! they were all withered and yellow. It was in a corner that he lay, among weeds and nettles. The golden star of tinsel was still on the top of the Tree, and glittered in the sunshine.

In the courtyard some of the merry children were playing who had danced at Christmas round the Fir tree, and were so glad at the sight of him. One of the youngest ran and tore off the golden star.

"Only look what is still on the ugly old Christmas tree!" said he, trampling on the branches, so that they all cracked beneath his feet.

And the Tree beheld all the beauty of the flowers, and the freshness in the garden; he beheld himself, and wished he had remained in his dark corner in the loft; he thought of his first youth in the woods, of the merry Christmas Eve, and of the little Mice who had listened with so much pleasure to the story of Klumpy-Dumpy.

"'Tis over—'tis past!" said the poor Tree. "Had I but rejoiced when I had reason to do so! But now 'tis past, 'tis past!"

And the gardener's boy chopped the Tree into small pieces; there was a whole heap lying there. The wood flamed up splendidly under the large brewing copper, and it sighed so deeply! Each sigh was like a shot.

The boys played about in the court, and the youngest wore the gold star on his breast which the Tree had had on the happiest evening of his life. However, that was over now—the Tree was gone, the story at an end. All, all was over; every tale must end at last.

CHRISTMAS AT THUNDER GAP*

By Katharine O. Wright

OUTSIDE the tall, clear window a star hung in the blue Kentucky evening. It shone into the church-house upon Mary, singing to her Babe in the straw—and Stacy Ellen, peeping through the cedar boughs that made the whole place sweet, caught her breath at the scene. There came the shepherds, wearing striped homespun, and there the kings and wise men, bearing gifts. That "Least One" reminded Stacy Ellen of the baby sister she'd be seeing tomorrow when she went home up Thunder Gap. Because of the baby, she had almost run away last autumn, soon after Pappy had left her in the school. It had been hard enough leaving Pappy and Mammy and the five young-uns—but leaving the Least One, whom she had loved and tended from birth, had been almost more than she could bear.

Now she glanced with ecstatic eyes across the swelling music, beyond the light that shone from the manger, to the faces of the other boys and girls uplifted in the half darkness of the church-house, and wondered if they were half as happy as she. Was this really Stacy Ellen of Thunder Gap, wearing a flowing robe, a blue ribbon holding the dark hair off her forehead? She pinched one hard little hand beneath its flowing sleeve. Yes! It was Stacy Ellen all right, seeing the Christmas play at the settlement for the first time, and taking part in it, too. Heaving a sigh of contentment, she thought, "I'm glad now I tromped on my homesickness for the sake o' larnin'."

Peeping through the cedar boughs, she forgot she had never

* Reprinted by permission of the AMERICAN GIRL, a magazine published by Girl Scouts.

worn a ribbon before; she almost forgot to sing with the other angels! Then her voice welled up with theirs:

"*Glory, in the highest, glory,*
"*Peace on earth, good will toward men!*"

As she sang, longing swept over her to take Christmas home to Thunder Gap. But, lawsy, there wouldn't be much chance for Christmas at home. Mammy was so busy with a houseful of young-uns and Pap had his hands full feeding and clothing them, not to mention helping send her to school.

Later, the whole school trooped out into the starry night to receive gifts from a growing hemlock tree that blossomed with red, gold, and blue lights. What a sight, what a sight! The shadowy mountains rising about the dark valley, and the glory of the lighted tree; all the young-uns shouting and singing and unwrapping presents. Stacy Ellen received a beautiful box of handkerchiefs, a box of pencils, and a whole box of candy. It was marvelous, and she stifled an unruly longing for another tree—a tree that would bear gifts for Mammy, Pappy, the five, and the Least One, up Thunder Gap.

"Good night! Merry Christmas!" the boys and girls shouted when the last package had been unwrapped, for to-morrow they'd be starting home with the rising of the sun.

In her tiny room Stacy Ellen smiled as she drew her blue robe over her dark hair, and carefully folded her ribbon. "With mighty nigh a week to ponder, 'pears like a body as chock full o' Christmas as I am ought to think up something!" she told the starry night.

Next morning, at the crack of dawn, she tied her braid with its usual string, packed her possessions in a bundle and fastened it, with her best shoes, on the end of a stick. After she had helped with the breakfast dishes—for she worked her way in the school— she donned her old brown coat and red cap and started out, hoisting her bundle-stick gunwise over her shoulder. Closing the big gate across the road, she climbed up on its bars a moment to look at the pretty houses of log and green wood scattered over the valley. Her eye followed the chimney smoke, up and up, to the top of the ridge that rose like a wall behind the school. The sunball was just looking over, and its rays lay up there like a golden veil caught in the bare branches of timber.

"I'll have to come back," she told herself wistfully. "Three months ain't near enough to git larnin'." Then she jumped off the gate bar and ran after the other boys and girls.

There were eight of them going her way, but gradually they parted company, some to go up one creek, some down another. Stacy Ellen felt lucky. She had only eighteen miles to walk and all day to walk it. The tall, long-legged boy who strode beside her had fifty miles to go, and would spend to-night at his Uncle's, part way. They all had some such journey to make and thought little of it.

"Ye're the fastest-walkingest boy I ever did see, Zack!" Stacy Ellen announced to the long-legged one, and he slackened his pace and looked down at her.

"However will ye git home so far by your lonesome?" he inquired.

"It's easy," she told him. "All I do is follow this creek to where Yancy Creek flows into it. I follow Yancy to its water-shed, and t'other side the ridge I'll find a spring that is the headwaters o' Crazy Creek. Crazy does a sight o' wanderin', but it'll lead me home!" She had a determined look in her blue eyes.

The boy gazed at her with admiration, "Ye'll git thar," he said.

The creek they walked beside shuttled through the mountains so that it was sometimes hard telling which was east, which west. Now the sun shone on the brown water before them, now it glanced from rhododendron leaves behind them, but they trusted that creek, and, with true mountaineer instinct, followed it through the wilderness. At last it was the turn of the long-legged boy to strike out over a high ridge.

"Whoo-ee-ee!" From the summit he called down the "sang cry" to Stacy Ellen.

"Whoo-ee-ee!" she flung back the old cry her grandparents had used when out gathering ginseng, because it carried through the mountains further than any other.

When the call was a mere echo from the ridge top, Stacy Ellen was alone in the wilderness. She walked along, her bundle bobbing behind her red cap. Now that she was by herself, she could plan some way to share Christmas with the folks at Thunder Gap.

"It's harder than nine times seven, take away five, carry three!" she sighed, wrinkling her brow.

In her bundle she had tucked one of the handkerchiefs for Mammy, and a pencil for Pappy, and there was the candy for the young-uns. But, lawsy! What was one little box of candy? Why, Aaron, her next oldest brother, could eat it in a few mouthfuls. She longed to have a new calico dress for Mammy, and some play toys for the young-uns—and Pap—he'd hankered after a flash light for a month o' Sundays! Picking her precarious way across foot logs and rolling rocks that might have thrown her into the creek, she pondered about Christmas.

Presently she heard a roar ahead of her and knew that Yancy was pouring its waters into the creek beside her. Hurrah! That was where she turned off to cross the ridge. The sun-ball was straight overhead when she bent her back and started up the steep slope. As she climbed, her bundle stick cut first into one shoulder, and then into the other, as she shifted it, and her face grew warm and red as her cap. After two hours she reached the watershed and looked down the other side of the mountain. Somewhere in the tangle of valleys far below was home—Thunder Gap. A lump came into her dry throat.

Dropping down beside the tiny spring that was the headwaters of Crazy Creek, she ate her lunch, still pondering her problem. Of course, she could make a wreath for the fireboard, a lovely wreath such as she had learned to make at school; and then there might be sorghum molasses taffy—happen Mammy could spare the 'lasses. She had not got far with her plans when she noticed that the sun was sliding down the sky. Jumping up, she followed the silver trickle from the spring, down and down, its voice growing louder until it became Crazy Creek, a wild torrent in a hemlock gorge. Darkness lurked beside it, and, by the time Stacy Ellen's foot touched the bottom land, she cast a shadow in moonlight. She was tired, but she felt safe now, for she knew every step of the way. It was all so peaceful in the bottom land; hayricks seemed resting for the night, and she liked to hear the satisfied cluck of the chickens as they roosted in the trees. Far ahead, up the Gap, she saw a light, and knew that Mammy had left the door open to welcome her.

"That you, leetle gal?" a voice called. It was Pappy, come to meet her.

Mammy made a silhouette against the firelight in the doorway, the Least One in the crook of her arm. The five young-uns hugged Stacy Ellen and took on, but Mammy was the say-nothing kind. Only from the look of her eyes could Stacy Ellen tell how glad she was to have her oldest daughter, her right hand helper, home again. But the Least One had forgotten her! Tired as she was, that knowledge brought the tears to her eyes.

"Hit'll recollect ye again when ye frolic with hit," Mammy told her.

When she was fed, and sat warming herself before the hickory fire, Stacy Ellen put back her head and feasted her eyes on the circle around the hearth. Pappy, big and angular, Mammy, thin and tired-looking, Aaron, and Fairannie who had been named from a ballad-song, the twins—a handful to manage—little Tom, and the Least One whom they called Glory. Glory traveled from lap to lap, cooing, crowing, but avoiding Stacy Ellen. If only that provoking baby would not act so uppity!

Outside, the winter wind howled down Thunder Gap, but here, beside the fire, all was snug and safe. The fat pine crackled, glinting on red peppers and pumpkin that hung drying in the rafters. The patchwork on the poster bed looked gay, and so did the old indigo-blue "kiver" Grannie had woven. Stacy Ellen thought how pretty the cabin would be, all decked with greens. She answered Mammy's and Pappy's questions about the school, and, drowsy as she was, sang them the angels' song from the Christmas play. Then the Least One came creeping from lap to lap until she laughed up at Stacy Ellen who took the plump little body into her arms.

"How about takin' yore thumb outen yore mouth?" she enquired after a while. The Least One looked at her reproachfully, but surrendered the choice morsel into her keeping.

Next morning the family arose from bed a good hour before the sun was up, and huddled, dressing, before the fire Pappy had made. From the kitchen shed came the sound of sizzling, and the aroma of bacon and coffee. Mammy had been up ahead of them, wrestling with the wood stove.

Stacy Ellen saw to it that the young-uns washed behind their ears, then she caught up the milk bucket and went out to the barnyard. From where she milked she watched Pappy disappear up the logging trail, driving the mule critter hitched to the wood sledge. "He's going after Christmas trees to haul to town," she thought, as the milk hissed against the tin bucket beneath her capable hands. "He'll haul 'em over the new road the Gov'ment's building, and the money he'll get for the trees'll buy food to keep the folks till there's garden stuff in the spring o' the year. It'll pay my entrance fee back to school, too." Even though Stacy Ellen worked her way in the school, Pappy had to help some.

"But there won't be money to spend on Christmas," she told the cow, "and it ain't our way to have a Christmas tree." No, Pap would never think to bring his own young-uns a Christmas tree. But why not have one anyway? She looked around, past the cow, to see if she could find one. Down by the creek was a whole thicket of holly trees, and before the cabin door grew a single holly, slim, pointed, and crimson with berries. "The very thing!" she murmured, "but there's nothin' for to trim it!"

The cow chewed her cud complacently as though to agree, "No, there's nothing for to trim it."

It was a beautiful tree, but the young-uns were used to it, and it ought to be decked somehow for Christmas. Stacy Ellen longed for tinsel, and an angel to go on its top, and colored balls to reflect happy children's faces, but these were out of the question. Her arms dropped to her sides and she sat on her little stool, staring out at the horizon. Then suddenly she awoke to the fact that the milk bucket was full to overflowing, and that the cow was looking around at her as though to enquire, "What more do you want?"

The next minute all thought of Christmas was banished from Stacy Ellen, for, as she entered the doorway with the brimming bucket, a chicken ran between her legs, tripping her. The twins laughed and she saved the milk by a miraculous feat of juggling.

"What's that chicken doing in the house?" she demanded, and the twins told her joyously that it laid an egg for them every morning on the trundle bed.

"The very idea! Well, I'll larn it better!" the older sister scolded, as she shooed the hen out the door.

The cabin was in confusion. From the kitchen shed came the "swish, swish," of Mammy's churn, and the young-uns were amusing themselves as they pleased. Aaron had let the fire go out, so that a patch of cold daylight fell down the chimney into the ashes. The peppers, which had caught the firelight last night, looked gray against the smoky rafters, the beds were unmade, and little Tom pulled about a chair, to which the Least One clung, staggering.

"I'm larnin' hit to walk," he announced.

"Well, don't pull so fast! Hit's legs'll give out," Stacy Ellen warned, feeling Christmas far, far away. She stepped out the door and drew a deep breath of the cold mountain air. Whatever could she do? Then she stepped in again.

"How'd ye like to deck this yere house for Christmas?"

The young-uns were puzzled. "How deck it?" they inquired.

"Oh, hang it with greens and suchlike."

Aaron looked dumbfounded. "They's some turnip greens in the garden," he told her doubtfully, "but they's froze."

"Holly and sichlike pretties!" she explained. And then the young-uns became interested and demanded to know more.

"If ye want to git ready for Christmas," she told them, "ye'll have to pitch in and clean up this shack within an inch o' its life—and, mind ye, it's got to shine before I tell ye any more about Christmas."

Immediately began such a scurrying to and fro that she had to stop them. "Wait!" she cried. "Aaron, you take out the ashes and lay the fire. Here, Fairannie, you sweep." She thrust a cornshuck broom into the child's hand. "Tom, you kin mind the Least One, while one twin helps me make the beds, and t'other brings in kindlin' wood."

From that moment they were so busy that Mammy, when she came in from the kitchen shed, stood amazed at the order and cleanliness she beheld.

"Now," said Stacy Ellen to the row of young-uns, "we kin begin to think about Christmas. Aaron, ye kin knock to pieces yan old barrel in the barnyard, and bring me the wire hoops. The rest o' ye pull on yore coats and come with me."

Taking a knife, she went down to the holly thicket beside the creek and cut some beautiful twigs with berries, which she dropped into the hemp sack Fairannie held open. Next she led the young-uns up through the frozen cornfield, where, perched on the snake fence, she cut twigs from the slim pointed cedar trees. Their berries were blue as the evening sky she had seen through the church-house window. Last she gathered hemlock branches with cones like tiny, brown roses. All these she carried back to the cabin, and there, before the fire, she bound twig above twig on the wire hoop until, beneath her resin-stained fingers, lay a beautiful wreath. The young-uns watched, breathless with interest, handing her now a bit of holly, now a string to tie it, and now a cluster of cones. When the wreath was done, Stacy Ellen held it up.

"I orter have a red ribbon for it," she said critically.

"How'd a bunch o' my red peppers do?" Mammy inquired, for she had come in to admire.

"The very thing!" Stacy Ellen exclaimed, and, when she had fastened the gay red in the green, she hung the wreath on the gun peg above the fireboard. The young-uns shouted with glee, for suddenly their cabin had become festive, gala, capable of any Christmas possibility.

Stacy Ellen left Fairannie and the twins making a second wreath while she took Aaron outside and talked to him confidentially.

"I want some pretties of some kind to deck this holly tree while the young-uns are asleep night before Christmas," she told him. "Do ye reckon ye kin help me find some?"

Aaron wrinkled his freckled nose, and then remembered that he had a treasure box hidden under the house, behind the chimney.

"I 'low thar'll be something I could loan ye," he told his sister. "I have to keep the box hid so the young-uns won't finger my things."

With that, he dived out of sight and reappeared with a cigar box which, when opened, revealed eight feathers dropped by cardinal birds, six feathers from blue birds, and tiny feathers of the wild canary, some gay pebbles and a roll of tinfoil.

Stacy Ellen clapped her hands. "Lawsy, Aaron," she exclaimed, "if ye'd picked these for a Christmas tree, ye couldn't a-done better! We'll stick the tail feathers in the branches and wrop the tinfoil around sycamore balls. They'll be a sight, a-hangin' in the holly tree!"

Snatching a hickory basket, she ran into the woods for the sycamore balls, followed by Aaron. They found the seed pods of teasel, also, and milkweed, and a dried branch of persimmon. It was amazing how much color you could find in winter fields and woods if you just kept your eyes open!

She and Aaron had filled their basket when they heard a crashing sound up in the timber. Rocks came rolling down the trail, underbrush was breaking. They looked at each other. Whatever could it be? Then suddenly the mule critter came galloping down the trail, dragging his harness behind him. Where was Pappy and the wood sledge?

"Whoa, Jonah!" yelled Aaron, and the mule critter drew up abruptly. He was trembling and wild-eyed. Something dreadful must have happened up on the mountain.

Stacy Ellen's heart sank, and Aaron went so pale that his freckles stood out starkly.

"We've got to go find Pap," Stacy Ellen murmured, trembling.

"I reckon ye're right!" said Aaron, and, gathering up the reins, he turned the mule about. Leaving their basket and all thought of Christmas behind, they hurried up the mountain.

Strange, thought Stacy Ellen, that Jonah, the mule critter, always so greedy for food and stall at the end of the day, should now hurry back up the steep slope. Indeed, he went so fast that they had to stop him and climb on his back. Oh, whatever had happened to Pappy? They shouted for him at the top of their lungs, but the sighing of the wind in the trees high above them was their only answer. Stacy Ellen blinked back tears and Aaron bit his lips, as they clung to Jonah's back. He carried them up and up, lunging over rocks and roots until he had passed out of the timber belt, and into the balsam pines that girdled the mountain top. There, in a thicket, he stopped, and they jumped down, and looked about.

It was cold up there. A light snow covered the ground and the green boughs of the balsams. Aaron and Stacy Ellen ran about, shouting for Pappy.

In the snow, they found the tracks of sledge runners, and, following them, they discovered the sledge, overturned. It was loaded with Christmas trees which were tied with rope. Pappy had been ready to start down when something had happened. What was it— oh, what was it? Together they righted the sledge, shouting wildly.

"Be still, Aaron!" cried Stacy Ellen, suddenly. "I thought I heard something that time." A groan came to her from beneath the ledge of rock where she stood. Fearfully they peered over it and saw Pappy lying with his foot jammed between two stones.

"That ye, leetle gal?" he murmured feebly. "I 'lowed ye'd come! I slipped and a rock rolled on my foot. It's broke or sprained. Try—" But Pappy got no further. His eyes closed with the pain.

Stacy Ellen hardly knew how she and Aaron climbed down and

dislodged the heavy bowlder, but they did, and then came a greater difficulty. Pappy could not bear to have his foot touched. How could they ever get him up the sloping rock to the sledge? He solved the problem himself, easing his weight with one foot, holding to Stacy Ellen and Aaron with his arms, and dragging the injured foot. It was an agonizing process, but at last he reclined on the balsam bed made by rearranging the trees on the sledge. By the time Aaron had rehitched the mule, a faint smile came to his lips.

"Good old Jonah," he said to the animal. "I heerd ye break loose and overturn the sledge, but I didn't 'low ye had gumption enough to bring help!"

"Mules are smart critters though they be stubborn sometimes!" observed Aaron as they started their painful way down the rough trail. He walked, leading Jonah, while Stacy Ellen kept pace with the sledge, helping to support Pappy. It seemed to them that Jonah picked his way over roots and stones with extra care. After a long, long time they drew up before the cabin door.

When Mammy had overcome her first fright, she took charge and they got Pappy into the house; then Aaron unhitched the mule and galloped away over the new road for the doctor. It was two hours before he could get there, but he reassured them after examining the foot. It was badly sprained and bruised, but not broken. Pappy would have to stay off it at least two weeks. When Mammy had paid the small fee the doctor asked there was little left to jingle in the money box.

Stacy Ellen knew it was not pain that made Pappy look so unhappy now. It was worry. The sale of his trees in town would have brought money to keep them in food till the spring of the year, when he could work on the new road and make a garden. How could they get on, these worst months of winter, without that money?

"A body can't jest set still and take sich trouble!" she told herself, squaring her small chin. Then she burst out, "Pappy, why can't Aaron and I haul those trees to town? Ye could tell us what to do with 'em!"

Pappy looked at her hopelessly. They wouldn't know how to sell the trees, he said. No, he couldn't see their going.

"Ye needn't think I'm the homesick young-un ye took to school last fall, Pappy!" Stacy Ellen cried. "I'm full growed now, and able to take keer o' myself. I jest know Aaron and I kin sell those trees."

Something about the look of her convinced Pappy. Hope came into his eyes, and he sat up, gazing at his daughter as though he saw her for the first time. "All right!" he said, "Go ahead and try!"

All at once it seemed to Stacy Ellen that the cabin was filled with Christmas. The scent of cedar in the fire warmth was part of it; and part of it was Mammy who was holding the Least One and suddenly began to sing an old Christmas ballad about Joseph, and a cherry tree that bowed down its branches so that Mary might pluck its fruit. The young-uns gathered 'round to listen. When the song was ended, Pappy glanced up and noticed the wreath for the first time. He complimented Stacy Ellen and remarked that town folks would like wreaths like that.

"Why not make some this evenin', an' take 'em along with the trees?" she suggested.

And that was how it happened that she and Aaron forgot how tired they were, and Pappy forgot his pain, making wreaths until the old clock on the fireboard struck midnight. It was a great stack of them that Stacy Ellen lifted out on the cold porch before they went to bed.

It snowed while they slept and, next morning, Stacy Ellen and Aaron had to shake the white from the trees before they reloaded them in the jolt wagon. A dozen beautiful wreaths they tucked between. Then, after Pappy had given last instructions, they flicked Jonah with the reins and drove away, crushing crystal grasses in the creek bed, tracking the snowy road to town. It was a long ride, but the cold, sunlit air was glorious, and town itself was a thrilling adventure. Perched on the high spring seat above their greenery, they looked down upon people, traffic, and dooryards, while the mule critter pulled them up one street and down another.

Success beyond their dreams awaited Stacy Ellen and Aaron. Because their trees were symmetrical and sturdy, people wanted them. And because the wreaths were unusual, as well as beautiful, they sold like hot cakes at a dollar apiece.

"I think we might take a leetle o' the wreath money," said Stacy Ellen at last, when the wagon was empty and the money box full, "and git some presents for the folks at home." So they bought a length of pretty calico for Mammy, a flash light for Pappy, and a play-toy for each of the young-uns. Stacy Ellen insisted that Aaron select the jackknife he had coveted so long, and they lingered with delight over the purchase of a small woolly lamb for the Least One.

It seemed to them both that they had never been so happy as they were, driving home over the snowy mountains.

"There'll be the tree all trimmed when the young-uns open the door in the morning," Stacy Ellen told Aaron, blissfully. "Then we can make pull-taffy and popcorn balls. And we'll ask Mammy to sing that cherry tree song again about Mary and Joseph and the leetle Jesus. 'Pears like I never knew what a lovely song that were before. I'll take that back to the school! They favor sich old song-ballads there, and put 'em in books!"

THE FESTIVAL OF SAINT NICHOLAS

By MARY MAPES DODGE

WE ALL know how, before the Christmas tree began to flourish in the home-life of our country, a certain "right jolly old elf," with "eight tiny reindeer," used to drive his sleigh-load of toys up to our housetops, and then bound down the chimney to fill the stockings so hopefully hung by the fireplace. His friends called him Santa Claus; and those who were most intimate ventured to say, "Old Nick." It was said that he originally came from Holland. Doubtless he did; but, if so, he certainly, like many other foreigners, changed his ways very much after landing upon our shores. In Holland, Saint Nicholas is a veritable saint, and often appears in full costume, with his embroidered robes glittering with gems and gold, his mitre, his crosier, and his jewelled gloves. Here Santa Claus comes rollicking along on the 25th of December, our holy Christmas morn; but in Holland, Saint Nicholas visits earth on the 5th, a time especially appropriated to him. Early on the morning of the 6th, which is Saint Nicholas Day, he distributes his candies, toys, and treasures, and then vanishes for a year.

Christmas Day is devoted by the Hollanders to churchrites and pleasant family visiting. It is on Saint Nicholas Eve that their young people become half wild with joy and expectation. To some of them it is a sorry time; for the saint is very candid, and, if any of them have been bad during the past year, he is quite sure to tell them so. Sometimes he carries a birch-rod under his arm, and advises the parents to give them scoldings in place of confections, and floggings instead of toys.

It was well that the boys hastened to their abodes on that bright winter evening; for, in less than an hour afterwards, the saint made his appearance in half the homes of Holland. He visited the king's palace, and in the selfsame moment appeared in Annie Bouman's comfortable home. Probably one of our silver half-dollars would have purchased all that his saintship left at the peasant Bouman's. But a half-dollar's worth will sometimes do for the poor what hundreds of dollars may fail to do for the rich: it makes them happy and grateful, fills them with new peace and love.

Hilda van Gleck's little brothers and sisters were in a high state of excitement that night. They had been admitted into the grand parlor: they were dressed in their best, and had been given two cakes apiece at supper. Hilda was as joyous as any. Why not? Saint Nicholas would never cross a girl of fourteen from his list, just because she was tall and looked almost like a woman. On the contrary, he would probably exert himself to do honor to such an august-looking damsel. Who could tell? So she sported and laughed and danced as gayly as the youngest, and was the soul of all their merry games. Father, mother, and grandmother looked on approvingly; so did grandfather, before he spread his large red handkerchief over his face, leaving only the top of his skull-cap visible. This kerchief was his ensign of sleep.

Earlier in the evening, all had joined in the fun. In the general hilarity, there had seemed to be a difference only in bulk between grandfather and the baby. Indeed, a shade of solemn expectation, now and then flitting across the faces of the younger members, had made them seem rather more thoughtful than their elders.

Now the spirit of fun reigned supreme. The very flames danced and capered in the polished grate. A pair of prim candles, that had been staring at the astral lamp, began to wink at other candles far away in the mirrors. There was a long bell-rope suspended from the ceiling in the corner, made of glass beads, netted over a cord nearly as thick as your wrist. It generally hung in the shadow, and made no sign; but tonight it twinkled from end to end. Its handle of crimson glass sent reckless dashes of red at the papered wall, turning its dainty blue stripes into purple. Passers-by halted to catch the merry laughter floating through curtain and sash into the street, then skipped on their way with the startled consciousness that the village was wide awake. At last matters grew so uproarious that the grandsire's red kerchief came down from his face with a jerk. What decent old gentleman could sleep in such a racket! Mynheer van Gleck regarded his children with astonishment. The baby even showed symptoms of hysterics. It was high time to attend to business. Mevrouw suggested that, if they wished to see the good Saint Nicholas, they should sing the same loving invitation that had brought him the year before.

The baby stared, and thrust his fist into his mouth, as mynheer put him down upon the floor. Soon he sat erect, and looked with a sweet scowl at the company. With his lace and embroideries, and his crown of blue ribbon and whalebone (for he was not quite past the tumbling age), he looked like the king of the babies.

The other children, each holding a pretty willow basket, formed at once in a ring, and moved slowly around the little fellow, lifting their eyes meanwhile; for the saint to whom they were about to address themselves was yet in mysterious quarters.

Mevrouw commenced playing softly upon the piano; soon the voices rose—gentle, youthful voices, rendered all the sweeter for their tremor—

"Welcome, friend! Saint Nicholas, welcome!
Bring no rod for us tonight!
While our voices bid thee welcome,
Every heart with joy is light.

"Tell us every fault and failing;
We will bear thy keenest railing
So we sing, so we sing:
Thou shalt tell us everything!

"Welcome, friend! Saint Nicholas, welcome!
Welcome to this merry band!
Happy children greet thee, welcome!
Thou art gladdening all the land.

"Fill each empty hand and basket;
'Tis thy little ones who ask it.
So we sing, so we sing:
Thou wilt bring us everything!"

During the chorus, sundry glances, half in eagerness, half in dread, had been cast towards the polished folding-doors. Now a loud knocking was heard. The circle was broken in an instant. Some of the little ones, with a strange mixture of fear and delight, pressed against their mother's knee. Grandfather bent forward, with his chin resting upon his hand; grandmother lifted her spectacles; Mynheer van Gleck, seated by the fireplace, slowly drew his meerschaum from his mouth; while Hilda and the other children settled themselves beside him in an expectant group.

The knocking was heard again.

"Come in," said the mevrouw, softly.

The door slowly opened; and Saint Nicholas, in full array, stood before them. You could have heard a pin drop. Soon he spoke. What a mysterious majesty in his voice! what kindliness in his tones!

"Karel van Gleck, I am pleased to greet thee, and thy honored vrouw, Kathrine, and thy son, and his good vrouw, Annie.

"Children, I greet ye all—Hendrick, Hilda, Broom, Katy, Huygens, and Lucretia. And thy cousins—Wolfert, Diedrich, Mayken, Voost, and Katrina. Good children ye have been, in the main, since I last accosted ye. Diedrich was rude at the Haarlem fair last fall; but he has tried to atone for it since. Mayken has failed, of late, in her lessons; and too many sweets and trifles have gone to her lips, and too few strivers to her charity-box. Diedrich, I trust, will be a polite, manly boy for the future; and Mayken will endeavor to shine as a student. Let her remember, too, that economy and thrift are needed in the foundation of a worthy and generous life. Little Katy has been cruel to the cat more than once. Saint Nicholas can hear the cat cry when its tail is pulled. I will forgive her, if she will remember from this hour that the smallest dumb creatures have feeling, and must not be abused."

As Katy burst into a frightened cry, the saint graciously remained silent until she was soothed.

"Master Broom," he resumed, "I warn thee that boys who are in the habit of putting snuff upon the foot-stove of the schoolmistress may one day be discovered, and receive a flogging—" (Master Broom colored, and stared in great astonishment.) "But, thou art such an excellent scholar, I shall make thee no further reproof.

"Thou, Hendrick, didst distinguish thyself in the archery match last spring, and hit the doel, though the bird was swung before it to unsteady thine eye. I give thee credit for excelling in manly sport and exercise; though I must not unduly countenance thy boat-racing, since it leaves thee too little time for thy proper studies.

"Lucretia and Hilda shall have a blessed sleep tonight. The consciousness of kindness to the poor, devotion in their souls, and cheerful hearty obedience to household rule, will render them happy.

"With one and all I avow myself well content. Goodness, industry, benevolence, and thrift have prevailed in your midst. Therefore, my blessing upon you; and may the New Year find all treading the paths of obedience, wisdom, and love! Tomorrow you shall find more substantial proofs that I have been in your home. Farewell!"

With these words came a great shower of sugar-plums upon a linen sheet spread out in front of the doors. A general scramble followed. The children fairly tumbled over each other in their eagerness to fill their baskets. Mevrouw cautiously held the baby down upon the sheet while the chubby little fists were filled. Then the bravest of the youngsters sprang up and threw open the closed doors. In vain they searched the mysterious apartment. Saint Nicholas was nowhere to be seen.

Soon they all sped to another room, where stood a table, covered with the whitest of linen damask. Each child, in a flutter of pleasure, laid a shoe upon it, and each shoe held a little hay for the good saint's horse. The door was then carefully locked, and its key hidden in the mother's bedroom. Next followed goodnight kisses, a grand family procession to the upper floor, merry farewells at bedroom doors, and silence, at last, reigned in the Van Gleck mansion.

Early the next morning, the door was solemnly unlocked and opened in the presence of the assembled household; when, lo! a sight appeared, proving good Saint Nicholas to be a saint of his word.

Every shoe was filled to overflowing; and beside each stood a many-colored pile. The table was heavy with its load of presents—candies, toys, trinkets, books, and other articles. Every one had gifts, from grandfather, down to the baby.

Little Katy clapped her hands with glee, and vowed inwardly that the cat should never know another moment's grief.

Hendrick capered about the room, flourishing a superb bow and arrows over his head. Hilda laughed with delight as she opened a crimson box, and drew forth its glittering contents. The rest chuckled, and said, "Oh!" and "Ah!" over their treasures, very much as we did here in America on last Christmas Day.

THE NIGHT BEFORE CHRISTMAS

By CLEMENT C. MOORE

'Twas the night before Christmas, when all through the house
Not a creature was stirring, not even a mouse;
The stockings were hung by the chimney with care,
In hopes that ST. NICHOLAS soon would be there;

The children were nestled all snug in their beds,
While visions of sugar-plums danced through their heads;
And Mamma in her 'kerchief, and I in my cap,
Had just settled our brains for a long winter's nap,—

When out on the lawn there arose such a clatter,
I sprang from my bed to see what was the matter;
Away to the window I flew like a flash,
Tore open the shutters and threw up the sash.

The moon on the breast of the new-fallen snow
Gave the lustre of mid-day to objects below;
When, what to my wondering eyes should appear,
But a miniature sleigh, and eight tiny reindeer,

With a little old driver, so lively and quick,
I knew in a moment it must be SAINT NICK.
More rapid than eagles his coursers they came,
And he whistled, and shouted, and called them by name:

"Now, *Dasher!* now, *Dancer!* now, *Prancer* and *Vixen!*
On, *Comet!* on, *Cupid* on, *Donder* and *Blitzen!*
To the top of the porch! to the top of the wall!
Now, dash away! dash away! dash away all!"

As dry leaves that before the wild hurricane fly,
When they meet with an obstacle, mount to the sky,
So up to the house-top the coursers they flew,
With a sleigh full of toys—and St. Nicholas too!

And then, in a twinkling, I heard on the roof,
The prancing and pawing of each little hoof.
As I drew in my head, and was turning around,
Down the chimney St. Nicholas came with a bound.

He was dressed all in fur, his head to his foot,
And his clothes were all tarnished with ashes and soot!
A bundle of toys he had flung on his back,
And he looked like a pedlar just opening his pack;

His eyes—how they twinkled! his dimples, how merry!
His cheeks were like roses, his nose like a cherry!
His droll little mouth was drawn up like a bow,
And the beard of his chin was as white as the snow.

The stump of a pipe he held tight in his teeth,
And the smoke, it encircled his head like a wreath.
He had a broad face, and a little round belly,
That shook, when he laugh'd, like a bowl full of jelly.

He was chubby and plump; a right jolly old elf;
And I laughed, when I saw him, in spite of myself.
A wink of his eye, and a twist of his head,
Soon gave me to know I had nothing to dread.

He spoke not a word, but went straight to his work,
And filled all the stockings—then turned with a jerk,
And laying his finger aside of his nose,
And giving a nod, up the chimney he rose.

He sprang to his sleigh, to his team gave a whistle,
And away they all flew, like the down off a thistle.
But I heard him exclaim, ere he drove out of sight,
"Happy Christmas to all! and to all a good night!"

HEIGH HO, THE HOLLY!

Blow, blow, thou winter wind,
Thou art not so unkind
   As man's ingratitude;
Thy tooth is not so keen,
Because thou art not seen,
   Although thy breath be rude.
Heigh ho, sing heigh ho, unto the green holly;
Most friendship is feigning, most loving mere folly:
   Then, heigh ho, the holly!
   This life is most jolly.

Freeze, freeze, thou bitter sky,
That dost not bite so nigh
   As benefits forgot:
Though thou the waters warp,
Thy sting is not so sharp
   As friend remember'd not.
Heigh ho, sing heigh ho, unto the green holly:
Most friendship is feigning, most loving mere folly:
   Then, heigh ho, the holly!
   This life is most jolly.
William Shakespeare

MINSTRELS

The minstrels played their Christmas tune
　To-night beneath my cottage-eaves;
While, smitten by a lofty moon,
　The encircling laurels, thick with leaves,
Gave back a rich and dazzling sheen,
That overpowered their natural green.

Through hill and valley every breeze
　Had sunk to rest with folded wings:
Keen was the air, but could not freeze,
　Nor check, the music of the strings;
So stout and hardy were the band
That scraped the chords with strenuous hand.

And who but listened?—till was paid
　Respect to every inmate's claim,
The greeting given, the music played
　In honour of each household name,
Duly pronounced with lusty call,
And "Merry Christmas" wished to all.
　　　　　　　　　　William Wordsworth

VOICES IN THE MIST

The time draws near the birth of Christ:
   The moon is hid; the night is still;
   The Christmas bells from hill to hill
Answer each other in the mist.

Four voices of four hamlets round,
   From far and near, on mead and moor,
   Swell out and fail, as if a door
Were shut between me and the sound:

Each voice four changes on the wind,
   That now dilate, and now decrease,
   Peace and goodwill, goodwill and peace,
Peace and goodwill, to all mankind.

Alfred, Lord Tennyson

TO A CHILD

Go, pretty child, and bear this flower
Unto thy little Saviour,
And tell Him, by that bud now blown,
He is the Rose of Sharon known.
When thou hast said so, stick it there
Upon His bib or stomacher;
And tell Him, for good handsel too,
That thou hast brought a whistle new,
Made of a clean straight oaten reed,
To charm His cries at time of need.
Tell Him, for coral thou hast none,
But, if thou hadst, He should have one;
But poor thou art, and known to be
Even as moneyless as He.
Lastly, if thou canst win a kiss
From those mellifluous lips of His,
Then never take a second on,
To spoil the first impression.
Robert Herrick

LET US KNEEL WITH MARY MAID

Before the paling of the stars,
   Before the winter morn,
Before the earliest cockcrow,
   Jesus Christ was born:
Born in a stable,
   Cradled in a manger,
In the world His hands had made,
   Born a stranger.

Priest and king lay fast asleep
   In Jerusalem,
Young and old lay fast asleep
   In crowded Bethlehem:

Saint and angel, ox and ass,
   Kept a watch together,
Before the Christmas daybreak
   In the winter weather.

Jesus on His Mother's breast
   In the stable cold,
Spotless Lamb of God was He,
   Shepherd of the fold.
Let us kneel with Mary Maid,
   With Joseph bent and hoary,
With saint and angel, ox and ass,
   To hail the King of Glory.

Christina Rossetti

WHERE IS THE BABE?

Tell us, thou clear and heavenly tongue,
Where is the Babe but lately sprung?
Lies He the lily-banks among?

Or say if this new Birth of ours
Sleeps, laid within some ark of flowers,
Spangled with dew-light; thou canst clear
All doubts, and manifest the where.

Declare to us, bright star, if we shall seek
Him in the morning's blushing cheek,
Or search the beds of spices through,
To find him out?

Robert Herrick

I SING THE BIRTH

I sing the birth was born to-night,
The Author both of life and light;
    The angels so did sound it.
And like the ravish'd shepherds said,
Who saw the light, and were afraid,
Yet search'd, and true they found it.

The Son of God, th' Eternal King,
That did us all salvation bring,
    And freed the soul from danger;
He whom the whole world could not take,
The Word, which heaven and earth did make,
    Was now laid in a manger.

The Father's wisdom will'd it so,
The Son's obedience knew no No,
    Both wills were in one stature;
And as that wisdom had decreed,
The Word was now made flesh indeed,
    And took on Him our nature.

What comfort by Him do we win,
Who made Himself the price of sin,
    To make us heirs of glory,
To see this Babe, all innocence;
A martyr born in our defence:
    Can man forget this story?

Ben Jonson

THIS THE HAPPY MORN

This is the month, and this the happy morn,
Wherein the Son of Heaven's Eternal King,
Of wedded Maid and Virgin Mother born,
Our great redemption from above did bring;
For so the holy sages once did sing,
    That He our deadly forfeit should release,
And with His Father work us a perpetual peace.

That glorious form, that light insufferable,
And that far-beaming blaze of majesty,
Wherewith He wont at Heaven's high council-table
To sit the midst of Trinal Unity,
He laid aside, and, here with us to be,
    Forsook the courts of everlasting day,
And chose with us a darksome house of mortal clay.

Say, Heavenly Muse, shall not thy sacred vein
Afford a present to the Infant God?
Hast thou no verse, no hymn, or solemn strain,
To welcome Him to this His new abode,
Now while the heaven, by the sun's team untrod,
    Hath took no print of the approaching light,
And all the spangled host keep watch in squadrons bright?

See how from far upon the eastern road
The star-led wizards haste with odours sweet!
Oh! run; prevent them with thy humble ode,
And lay it lowly at His blessed feet;
Have thou the honour first thy Lord to greet,
    And join thy voice unto the Angel quire,
From out His secret altar touched with hallowed fire.

John Milton

STOP THIEF!

Come, guard this night the Christmas-pie,
That the thief, though ne'er so sly,
With his flesh-hooks, don't come nigh
 To catch it

From him who all alone sits there,
Having his eyes still in his ear,
And a deal of nightly fear,
 To watch it.
Robert Herrick

CHRISTMAS—1863

I hear the bells on Christmas Day
The old familiar carols play,
   And wild and sweet,
   The words repeat
Of peace on earth, good-will to men.

Then from each black, accursed mouth
The cannon thundered in the South;
   And with that sound
   The carols drowned
Of peace on earth, good-will to men.

It was as if an earthquake rent
The hearthstones of a continent,
   And made forlorn
   The household born
Of peace on earth, good-will to men.

And in despair I bowed my head,
"There is no peace on earth," I said,
   "For hate is strong
   And mocks the song
Of peace on earth, good-will to men."

Then pealed the bells more loud and deep;
"God is not dead, nor doth He sleep;
   The Wrong shall fail,
   The Right prevail,
With peace on earth, good-will to men."
                     Henry Wadsworth Longfellow

INDEX

Adalbert, Archbishop of Bremen, 13
Adam, Adolphe, Belgian composer, 34
Adeste Fideles, 94
Agricultural rites, 17, 19, 26
Aguinaldos in Dominican Republic, 35
Albert, Prince-Consort, and Christmas trees, 7
Alexander, Cecil Frances, 101
American Girl, 37, 187
Amoli de Guajalote (Mexican roast turkey), 78
An, Le Jour de l', 13
Andersen, Hans Christian, 168
Angel Food Cake, Yellow, 81
Animal, Your Favorite, a game, 57, 64
Animals at Christmas, customs and superstitions, 17, 20, 22
Animals, Christmas, a game, 43
Anjou, Duc d', 10
Antioch, tune, 88, 95
Apples and Christmas, 26, 53
Appo, the Italian yule log, 29
Apricot and Rice Pudding, Frozen, 81
Art, Christmas, a game, 52
Ashen Fagot, at Dunster, England, 11
AT BRACEBRIDGE HALL, by Washington Irving, 160
Auction, Christmas Tree, 45
Austria, 88

Baldur the Beautiful, and mistletoe, 6
Ball Relay, Christmas, 61
Balloon Blowing Contest, 62
Banding the orchard trees with straw, 17
Barnyard, Christmas in the, a game, 63
Bavaria, as a toy-making district, 28
Bean in the cake, 13
Bee, Christmas, 48
Befana, St., 8, 15, 29
BELGIUM, 20, 34
Berlin, 28
Bevin Brothers Manufacturing Company, door bell makers, 73

Blessing of rivers, in Russia, 18
Boar's head, the, 10, 26, 55, 162
Book Show, a game, 69
Bottle the Popcorn, a game, 61
Boxing Day, 25, 26, 53
BRACEBRIDGE HALL, by Washington Irving, 160
Brady, Diamond Jim, 10
BRAZIL, 22, 35
Bread made on Christmas, 53
Brezaia celebration in Rumania, 33
Britain, 6; *see also* England
Brittle, Peanut, 84
Brooks, Phillips, 88, 98
Brownies, the, in Denmark, 32
Bubble Blowing Contest, 51
Buñuelos, Mexican Fried Puffs, 22, 79

Cablegrams, Christmas, a game, 47
Cake, Chocolate Surprise, 82
Cake, Fruit, 80
Cake, Mint Candy, 82
Cake, Yellow Angel Food, 81
CAKES AND PUDDINGS, CHRISTMAS, 80
Cakes, Cup, Gingerbread, 81
Cakes, German Christmas, 77
Cakes, Mexican, 78
CANDIES, CHRISTMAS, 83
Candle Relay Race, Christmas, 52
Candle Quoits, a game, 64
Carolers, 7
Carols, Christmas, the custom in various countries, 7, 12, 16, 25, 30, 31, 34, 35, 43, 55
CAROLS, CHRISTMAS, words and music, 87
Celaya, Mexico, 22
Cenone, the Italian Christmas Eve banquet, 29
Challengers, Contrary, a game, 46
Charity Fair, in Spain, 16
Chew Chew, a game, 63
Chickens and Christmas in Switzerland, 17

206

INDEX

Children, Parties and Games for, 55, 56
Children's Party, an Old-Fashioned, 56
Chimes, Christmas, a game, 50
Chocolate Rabbits, French, 76
Chocolate Surprise Cake, 82
Christkindli, 32
Christmas, its origin, history, etc., 5-6, 9, 13, 52, 54
Christmas Animals, a game, 43
Christmas Art, a game, 52
Christmas: A Definition, by Clement A. Miles, 156
Christmas at Thunder Gap, by Katharine O. Wright, 176
Christmas Ball Relay Race, 61
Christmas Bee, 48
Christmas Bells, 73
Christmas Cablegrams, a game, 47
Christmas Cakes and Puddings, 80
Christmas Cakes, German, 77
Christmas Candies, 83
Christmas Candle Relay Race, 52
Christmas Cards, Curving, a game, 50
"Christmas Carol" (Charles Dickens), a quiz, 48
CHRISTMAS CAROLS, 87; see also 7, 12, 25, 30, 31, 34, 35, 43, 55
Christmas "Chew Chew," a game, 63
Christmas Chimes, a game, 50
Christmas Concert, a stunt, 48
Christmas Cookies, French, 76
Christmas Dinner Menu, Mexican, 79
Christmas—1863, by Longfellow, 206
Christmas Eve, a carol, 92
Christmas Eve and Cupid, 17
Christmas Eve in France, 12, 76
Christmas Eve Supper Menu, French, 76
Christmas, Florida, a place, 52
Christmas Foxhunt, Warwickshire, 26, 53
Christmas Goat, Finland, 21
Christmas Greeting Cards, 8
Christmas 'If" Scavenger Hunt, 44
Christmas in Ritual and Tradition, 156
Christmas in the Barnyard, a game, 63
Christmas Island, a place, 52
Christmas Pantomime, stage plays, 12; a game, 45
CHRISTMAS PARTY, THE, 41
CHRISTMAS PLAYS, 105
Christmas Plum Pudding, a game, 63
CHRISTMAS POETRY AND STORIES, 155
Christmas Poetry, a game, 49

Christmas Pudding, English, 11
Christmas Punch, 85
Christmas Push, a stunt, 65
Christmas Quizzes, 48, 52, 58
Christmas, Religious Significance, 5
Christmas Roulette, a game, 64
Christmas Salad, 82
Christmas Scents, a game, 47
CHRISTMAS SCRAPBOOK, FROM A, 5
Christmas Seals, Concealed, a game, 49
Christmas Stocking, see Stocking
Christmas Stocking, Hanging the, a game, 58
CHRISTMAS STORY, THE GREATEST EVER TOLD, 1
Christmas, Symbols of, 5
CHRISTMAS TODAY IN OTHER LANDS, 25
Christmas Toy Shopping, a game, 47
Christmas Traditional Plays in Rumania, 19
Christmas Tree, see Tree
Christmas Tree Auction, a game, 45
Christmas Tree, Find the, a game, 57, 58
Christmas Tree, Trimming the, a game, 50
CHRISTMAS TREASURE, a play, 106
Christmas Word Game, 46
Chrysostom, St. John, 5
Church Decorations, 69
Church, Francis P., 157
Cider, a toast drunk to the apple tree, 26
Cole, Sir Henry, 8
Color Grab Bag Game, 59
Concealed Christmas Seals, a game, 49
Concert, Christmas, a stunt, 48
Contia, Russian dessert, 29
Cookies, French Christmas, 76
Contrary Christmas Challengers, 46
Courting at Christmas, 17
CRADLE HYMN, by Martin Luther, 88, 89
Cradle rocking of the little Jesus, 15
Crèche, see Crib sets
CRIB SCENE, decorations, etc., 70
Crib sets in various countries, 12, 16, 22, 34, 36
Crops, customs to assure good, in Switzerland, 17; in Rumania, 19
Cundall, Joseph, 8
Cup Cakes, Gingerbread, 81
Curving Christmas Cards, a game, 50
Cyril, St., 6

Day of Kings (Epiphany), 36
DECORATIONS, 69
DENMARK, 20, 31
Devil's Knell, at Dewsbury, 11
Dewsbury, 11
Diamond Jim Brady, 10
Diary, Holiday, a game, 51
Dickens, Charles, x, 26, 48
Dickens' "Christmas Carol" Quiz, 48
Dinner, Christmas Eve, and Christmas, in various lands, 29, 30, 31, 75, 76, 79, 80
Diocletian, Roman Emperor, 37
Dionysus worship, Rumanian relic of, 33
Divinity Fudge, 83
Do You Know? quiz, 53
Dodge, Mary Mapes, 188
Doll Shop, a game, 68
DOMINICAN REPUBLIC, 35
Doncaster, England, 11
Downey, Fairfax, 37
Drawing Contest, 68
Drink, a Temperance, 85
Drop Cakes (Platzen), 77
Druids, 6, 13
Dunster, Somersetshire, the Ashen Fagot, 11
Dutch, and Santa Claus, 8; see also Holland

Easy Christmas Poetry, a game, 49
Edward VI, and Christmas, 9
Egg breaking to tell fortunes, 18
Elizabeth, Queen, 9, 10
Elves, Christmas, in Finland, 30
Empanadas (Mexican cakes), 78
Engine Relay Race, 67
ENGLAND, 6, 7, 9, 11, 12, 25, 75
English Christmas Pudding, 11
English Turkey Stuffing, 75
Epiphany (Little Christmas, Old Christmas, Twelfth Day), 6, 8, 13, 15, 16, 19, 22, 29, 33, 35, 36; see also St. Befana
Erz Gebirge, toy-making district, 28
Eschenbach, Wolfram von, 7

Farm animals and Christmas, in various lands, 17, 20, 22, 32
Father Christmas, 12
Father Spanker, 12
Favorite Animal, Your, a stunt, 64
FESTIVAL OF SAINT NICHOLAS, by Mary Mapes Dodge, 188
Festival of the Kings, in France, 13

Fête des Rois, La, 13
Fill in the Missing Letters, a quiz, 54
Filling for German Marzipan, 77
Find the Christmas Tree, a game, 57, 58
FINLAND, 21, 30
FIR TREE, THE, by Hans Christian Andersen, 168
FIRST NOEL, THE, 100
Flight into Egypt, Rumania, 33
Florafilm, 72, 73
Fondant, Vanilla, 83
Forks in the Tudor period, 10
Fortune telling and good luck, 13, 15, 16, 17, 18, 19, 31, 80
Foster, Myles Birket, 92
Foxhunt, Warwickshire, England, 26, 53
FRANCE, 8, 12, 27, 76
Frankfort, Germany, 28
French alliance of Queen Elizabeth, proposed, 10
French carols—Noëls, 12, 87
French Chocolate Rabbits, 76
French Christmas Cookies, 76
French Réveillon or Christmas Eve Supper, Menu, 76
Fried Puffs (Mexican Buñuelos), 79
Frozen Fruit Salad, 82
Frozen Rice and Apricot Pudding, 81
Fruit Cake, 80
Fruit Salad, Frozen, 82
Fudge, Divinity, 83

Galette des Rois (a cake), 13
GAMES, 43
GAMES for Children, 43
GAMES for 4-to-6-year-olds, 58
——— 7-to-11-year-olds, 61
——— 12-to-15-year-olds, 63
GAMES AND PARTIES FOR CHILDREN, 55
Gauntlett, H. J., 101
German Christmas Cakes, 77
German Kristlieder, 87
GERMANY, 7, 8, 9, 13, 27, 54
Gift game, 51
Ginger Ale Salad, 83
Gingerbread Cup Cakes, 81
Girl Scouts, 187
Gloucestershire traditional Christmas plays, 26
Gnome of Good Luck, Swedish, 38
Goat, the Christmas, in Finland, 21
Goat's head, in Rumania, 33
GOD REST YOU MERRY, GENTLEMEN, 8, 102

INDEX 209

Gold Platters Preferred, 10
GOOD CHRISTIAN MEN, REJOICE, 103
GOOD KING WENCESLAS, 88, 91
Goodies to Eat, Belgian, 20
Grab Bag Game, Color, 59
Great Forest, Germany, 28
Grandfather Frost, in Russia, 30
GREATEST CHRISTMAS STORY EVER TOLD, 1
Greeting Cards, 8, 27
Gruber, Franz, 88, 97

Hampshire, traditional Christmas plays, 26
Handel, Georg Friedrich, 88, 95
Hanging the Christmas Stocking, a game, 58
HARK! THE HERALD ANGELS SING, 88, 96
Harper and Brothers, 69
Haxey Hood, near Doncaster, 11
HEIGH HO, THE HOLLY! by William Shakespeare, 196
Heil Holiday, 44, 57
Hengist and the wassail bowl, 11
Henry VIII, King, 9, 10
Herrick, Robert, 199, 201, 204
Holiday Diary, a game, 51
Holland, 9
Holy Trinity Church, Philadelphia, 88
HOME-COMING PARTY, THE, 42
HOME TABLE DECORATIONS, 71
Hoodlands, the, at Haxey, 11
Hopkins, Rev. John Henry, Jr., 88, 99
Horse racing in Finland, 21, 31

I SING THE BIRTH, by Ben Jonson, 202
ICE BREAKERS, 42, 43
"If" Scavenger Hunt, 44
Ignat (St. Ignatius' Day) in Rumania, 33
In a Much Lighter Vein! quiz, 54
INDOOR DECORATIONS, 73
Information Please, 11
Innocents, tune, 93
Irby, tune, 101
Irozii celebration in Rumania, 33
Irving, Washington, 160
IS THERE A SANTA CLAUS? by Francis P. Church, 157
IT CAME UPON THE MIDNIGHT CLEAR, 90
ITALY, 8, 15, 29

James I, King, 9
Jerusalem, Christmas at, 6
John Chrysostom, 5

Jonson, Ben, 202
Jour de l'An, 13
Jour de Noël, 12
JOY TO THE WORLD, 88, 95
Julenisse (the little Yule Dwarf) in Denmark, 20
Julius, Pope of Rome, 6
Jumping Jacks, a game, 69
Junior Christmas Quiz, 58

Kings, or Magi?, 53
Kings, Festival of the, in France, 13
Klaasjes (Belgian cake), 20
Kristlieder, 87
Kolyada songs, Russian, 87

Lapland, 21
LEGENDS AND CUSTOMS, 9
LET US KNEEL WITH MARY MAID, by Christina Rossetti, 200
Letterbanket (Belgian cake), 20
LIFE OF THE PARTY, THE, 48
Little Christmas (Epiphany), 36
London, 7, 12, 26
London *Times*, on greeting cards, 8
Long Christmas in Finland, 21
Longfellow, Henry Wadsworth, 206
Lord of Misrule, 10
Lucia, Saint, 37
Luther, Martin, 7, 14, 88, 89

Magi, the, 6, 13, 15, 16, 21, 29, 35, 36, 53
Magnus, Duke (later, King), 13
Making a Santa Claus, a game, 64
March of the Toys, a game, 67
Marsepein, Belgian traditions, 20
Marzipan, German, 77
Masquerade, *see* Mummers
Master of Merry Disports, 10
Maximilian, Emperor of Mexico, 22
Meeting the Magi, 16
Memoirs of an Editor, 157
Mendelssohn-Bartholdy, Felix, 96
Menu, Christmas, 30, 31, 75, 76, 79
"Merry Christmas" in many languages, 23
"Messiah, The," by Handel, 88
Mexican foods, 78, 79
MEXICO, 22, 36, 78, 79
Midnight Christmas Mass in various countries, 12, 16, 17, 29, 34, 35
Miles, Clement A., 156
Miller, Catherine Atkinson, 69
Milton, John, 203
Mince pie, 53

MINSTRELS, by William Wordsworth, 197
Mint Candy Cake, 82
Missa do Gallo (Midnight Mass), Brazil, 35
Missing Letters, quiz, 54, 55
Mistletoe, 6, 13
Mitchell, Edward P., 157
Mohr, Joseph, 88, 97
Montgomery, James, 93
Moore, Clement C., 9, 194
MRS. SANTA CLAUS' RECEPTION, 65
Mummers in various lands, 18, 21, 23, 26, 33, 55
Musical Wreath, a game, 57, 60
Mutton pies, old name for mince pies, 53

Nacimiento (Nativity crib), 16
Neale, John Mason, 88, 91, 103
Neva, blessing the river, 18
New Amsterdam, 8, 9
Newton, Sir Isaac, 53
New Year's Day, 10, 13, 27, 33, 35
New York, 8, 9
New York Sun, The, 157
Nicholas, *see* St. Nicholas, *and* Santa Claus
NIGHT BEFORE CHRISTMAS, THE, by Clement C. Moore, 194
Noche-Buena (Christmas Eve night) in Spain, 16
Noël, Le Jour de, 12
Noëls (carols), 12, 34, 87
Nuremburg, Germany, 28

O LITTLE TOWN OF BETHLEHEM, 88, 98
O SWEETEST NIGHT, by Myles Pinkney, 205
Oakley, F., 94
OH COME, ALL YE FAITHFUL, 94
O'Hanlon, Virginia, 157, 158
Old Christmas (Epiphany), 11
Old English Customs Still in Being, 11
OLD-FASHIONED CHILDREN'S PARTY, 56
Old-Fashioned Plum Pudding, 80
Old Man Christmas, in Finland, 21
Old Man with the Little Drum, German, 14
Old Spanish Towns, 16
Old Superstitions in Brazil, 22
Olney, Richard, 157
ONCE IN ROYAL DAVID'S CITY, 101
Onions and forecasting the weather for the year, 17
OUTDOOR DECORATIONS, 71

Oxfordshire, England, traditional Christmas plays, 26

Package, What's in the, a game, 60
Page, Thomas Nelson, 157
Pangiallo (Italian yellow bread), 29
Pantomimes, Christmas, stage plays, 12; a game, 45
Papa Noël in Brazil, 22, 35, 36
Parade of the Wooden Soldiers, a game, 69
Paris, France, 12, 27
PARTIES AND GAMES FOR CHILDREN, 55
PARTY FOR CHILDREN, AN OLD-FASHIONED, 56
PARTY, THE HOME-COMING, 42
PARTY, THE CHRISTMAS, 41
Pasadena, California, the winter Fête of Roses, 53
Peacock, the Christmas dish, 10
Peacock Pie, 163
Peanut Brittle, 84
Pear Salad, 83
PENCIL AND PAD PASTIMES, 46
Père Fouettard, Le, 12
Père Noël, 12
Petit Noël, Le, 12
Pfeffer-Nusse, 78
Philadelphia, Pennsylvania, 88
Pinkney, Myles, 205
Piñata, the, in Mexico, 36
Platzen (small German drop cakes), 77
PLAYS, CHRISTMAS, 105
Plum Pudding, Christmas, a game, 63
Plum Pudding, Old-Fashioned, 80
Plow, in Rumanian New Year's festivities, 33
POETRY AND STORIES, CHRISTMAS, 155
Poetry, Christmas, a game, 49
Popcorn Balls, 84
Popcorn, Bottle the, a game, 61
Popcorn Stringing, a game, 59
Posadas, in Mexico, 37
Presepe (Nativity crib or crèche) in Brazil, 22, 36
PUDDINGS AND CAKES, CHRISTMAS, 80
Pudding, the Christmas (English), 11
Pudding, Christmas Plum, a game, 63
Pudding, Frozen Rice and Apricot, 81
Pudding, Old-Fashioned Plum, 80
Punch, Christmas, 85
Puritans and Christmas, 52, 53
Pushing Apple through a Teacup, stunt, 65
Puzzle, a Santa, 61

INDEX 211

Queen Elizabeth, 9, 10
Queen Victoria, 7
Queen's College, Oxford, the Boar's head ceremony, 26, 55
Queretaro, Mexico, 22
QUIZZES, 48, 52, 58
Quoits, Candle, a game, 64

Rabbits, French Chocolate, 76
Reading, John, 94
Redner, Lewis H., 88, 98
REPRESHMENTS, 75
Relay Race, Christmas Ball, 61
Relay Race, Christmas Candle, 52
Relay Race, Engine, a game, 67
Religious Significance of Christmas, 5
REUNION AT CHRISTMAS, a play, 119
Réveillon Menu (French), 76
Rice and Apricot Pudding, Frozen, 81
Ring the Bell, a game, 59
Rings and Charcoal, to tell fortunes, 18
Risengrod (rice pudding), in Denmark, 20
Rivers, blessing of, in Russia, 18
Rois, La Fête des, 13
Römerberg, in Frankfort, Germany, 28
Rossetti, Christina, 200
Roulette, Christmas, a game, 64
Rowena, and the wassail bowl, 11
Rugby football; its supposed origin, 11
RUMANIA, 19, 33
Rural Christmas Customs in Switzerland, 17
RUSSIA, 18, 29, 30, 54, 87

SALADS, SEASONAL, 82
Saint, *see* St.
Santa, a puzzle, 61
Santa Claus, 8, 30, 32, 34, 35, 36, 57, 60, 66, 67, 157; *see also* St. Nicholas
Santa Claus, Indiana, a place, 52
Santa Claus, Making a, a game, 64
Santa's Helpers, a game, 62
Santa's Treat, a game, 60
Sauna (Finnish steam bath), 21, 30
Scandinavia, and the devotion to St. Lucy, 37
Scandinavian origin of various Christmas customs, 6
Scavenger Hunt, Christmas "If," 44
Scents, Christmas, a game, 47
SCHOOL DECORATIONS, 69
Scott, Sir Walter, 11
SCRAPBOOK, CHRISTMAS, FROM A, 5
Sears, Rev. Edmund H., 90

SEASONAL SALADS, 82
Shakespeare, William, 26, 196
Shepherds, Italian, 15; Rumanian, 19; Mexican, 23
Shoes instead of Christmas stockings, 8, 16, 20, 22, 34, 36
Shopping, Christmas Toy, a game, 47
SILENT NIGHT, 88, 97
Snow-Ball Throw, a game, 61
Soldiers, Parade of the Wooden, a game, 69
Solstice, the Winter, 6, 14
SONGS OF PRAISE THE ANGELS SANG, 93
SPAIN, 16
Spilman, J. E., 89
Stainer, Sir John, 103
St. Andrew's Day, 8
St. Befana, 8, 15, 29; *see also* Epiphany
St. Cyril, 6
St. Francis of Assisi, 36, 87
St. George and the Dragon, 55
St. Ignatius' Day, 33
St. John Chrysostom, 6
St. Lucy, 37
St. Nicholas of Myra, in various lands, 9, 20, 27, 32, 33, 34, 52, 54; *see also* Santa Claus
St. Paul's Cathedral, London, 7, 26
St. Stephen's Day (December 26), 21, 31, 53
St. Wenceslas, King of Bohemia, 88, 91
Star-Boys (mummers) in Finland, 21, 31
Stocking, Hanging the Christmas, a game, 58
Stockings, Christmas, 8, 35
Stoddard, Anne, 37
STOP THIEF! by Robert Herrick, 204
STORIES AND POETRY, CHRISTMAS, 155
Story Book Show, a game, 69
Stratford-on-Avon, Christmas mummers, 26
Straw ceilings, Finnish, 21
Stringing Popcorn, a game, 59
Stuffing, English Turkey, 75
Stunts, 48
"Stunts of All Lands," 69
Sun, The (New York), 157
Sunday, Christmas on, 53
Sunshine on Christmas, 53
Superstitions, 14, 22, 26, 32, 33, 53, 80; *see also* Fortune Telling
Surprise Cake, Chocolate, 82
SWEDEN, 37, 79
SWITZERLAND, 17, 32
SYMBOLS OF CHRISTMAS, 5

Table cutlery in Tudor period, 9
TABLE DECORATIONS, AT HOME, 71
Table manners in Tudor England, 9
Tähti Pojat (Star-Boys) in Finland, 31
Take Your Choice, a quiz, 53
Temperance Drink, Delightful, 85
Temple Church, London, 7, 26
Tennyson, Alfred, 198
Tensolite Laboratory, 72, 73
THIS THE HAPPY MORN, by John Milton, 203
Thor, and the yule log, 6
Three old customs of Finland, 21
Thuringia, as a toy-making district, 28
Times, London, on greeting cards, 8
TO A CHILD, by Robert Herrick, 199
Top Twirl, a game, 68
Torrone (Italian hard candy), 29
Toy Shopping, Christmas, a game, 47
Toys, German, 28
Tree, Christmas, 7, 14, 20, 22, 28, 30, 31, 32, 34, 37, 54, 69, 168
Tree, Auction, 45
Tree, Find the Christmas, a game, 57, 58
Trimming the Christmas tree, a game, 50
True or False Quiz, 52
Turkey, the Christmas, and English Kings, 9
Turkey, Mexican Roast, 78
Turkey Stuffing, English, 75
Tutanes (a British god) and the mistletoe, 6
Twelfth Day (Epiphany), 16
Twelfth Night, 10, 13, 21

Unpacking the Present, a game, 62
Unwin, T. Fisher, 156
Urn of Fate, in Italy and Spain, 15, 16

Vanilla Fondant, 83
Victoria, Queen, and Christmas trees, 7

VOICES IN THE MIST, by Alfred, Lord Tennyson, 198
Vortigern, and the wassail bowl, 11

Waits, the Christmas, 7, 12, 53
Waldteufel of cardboard, 28
Walnut Cream Drops, 84
Warwickshire traditional Christmas plays, 26
Wassail bowl, the, 11, 163
WATCHING IN THE MEADOWS (a carol), 92
Watts, Dr. Isaac, 88, 95
WE THREE KINGS OF ORIENT ARE, 88, 99
Weather forecast by an onion, 17
Wenceslas, King and Saint, 88, 91
Wesley, Charles, 88, 96
Wessex, battle, 11
Westminster Abbey, 7, 8, 26
What's in the Package, a game, 60
WHERE IS THE BABE? by Robert Herrick, 201
Willis, Richard S., 90
Winter solstice, 6, 14
Wise Men, *see* Magi
Witches frightened away, 14
Wolfram von Eschenbach, and Christmas trees, 7
Wooden Soldiers, Parade of the, a game, 69
Word Game, 46
Wordsworth, William, 197
Wreath, Musical, a game, 60
Wright, Katharine O., 176

Yellow Angel Food Cake, 81
Your Favorite Animal, a stunt, 64
Yule Dwarf, the Little (The Julenisse), Denmark, 20
Yule Log, 6, 7, 12, 26

Zelten (Belgian cakes), 20
Zurich, Switzerland, 33

DATE DUE

	DEC 2 3 1993		
DEC 1 4 1979		MAY 1 0 1995	
DEC 1 4 1979		NOV 1 8 1995	
1-15-80		MAY 0 6 1998	
		DEC 2 2 2005	
NOV 4 1981			
DEC 1 1982			
DEC 15 1982			
JAN 1 2 1983			
DEC 1 4			
DEC 1 0 1986			
DEC 0 6 1988			
DEC 1 3 1989			
MAY 0 9 1990			
DEC 1 1 1991			
DEC 2 1 1992			
MAY 1 2 1993			